GAME PLAN

Developing Intentional Missional Ministry

Tim Roehl

For Souls!
Tim Roehl
Psalm 126:5-6

Evangelism
& Church Growth

Indianapolis, IN

GAME PLAN

Developing Intentional Missional Ministry

Foreword

Missional has become a popular evangelical buzzword. It first came into use in the late 1990s through the influence of Bishop Lesslie Newbigin, a Scottish Presbyterian and missionary. Working and living in South India, Newbigin realized that the Church in Western countries is not really operating in a secular, rationalist environment with *no gods*, but rather in a spiritually pluralistic, pagan environment that offers *many false gods*—just like the situation it faces in a predominantly Hindu culture. So, the question becomes, "How do Christ-followers relate best to people who think they have many other spiritual options besides Him from which to choose?"

Being *missional* refers to a mindset focused on joining God in His mission of reconciling the world to Himself through Jesus Christ. It is an all-consuming task for the Church and its leaders. *Missional* is a great term for holiness evangelicals to use because we understand biblical discipleship and leadership as a call to voluntary, wholehearted commitment and loving, total submission to the lordship of Christ. Holiness evangelicals believe that, through the regenerating, purifying, empowering fullness of the Holy Spirit, God's people are able to love Him above all else, to love others with the full intensity of Christlike love, and to love doing His will in the world. We believe this kind of wholehearted, earnest discipleship is made possible by grace through faith in the regenerating, purifying, empowering fullness of the Holy Spirit. For us, being *missional* is intentionally living our individual and corporate lives to spread the transformational hope and holiness of Jesus Christ everywhere.

Play yourself a mental video for a moment. Imagine a beating, human heart. Watch it swell as it fills with freshly oxygenated blood; then contract to push that life force out in service to the entire body. Swelling and contracting. Filling and flowing. Gathering and sending.

You've just visualized how a missional church works. It gathers Christ-followers together, in order to inspire, equip, and then send them out in ministry to their families, friends, neighbors, and communities. Gathering and sending. Gathering and sending. That's the rhythm of a healthy congregation. We come together to be re-energized by God's Word, to receive fresh grace through the sacraments that Christ commanded us to observe, and to be reunited in the fellowship of the Holy Spirit. Then, compelled by God's love, we are sent out to share God's life-giving grace with our neighbors through our everyday words and deeds—all in hopes of persuading others to join us in becoming life-giving agents of God's grace, too.

The Church is the heart of God's mission, in which we mingle with other Christ-followers and from which we are then sent out to spread hope and holiness everywhere we can. Blood was never meant just to stay in the heart. If it does, it clots and kills. The missional church (whether local or collectively as a denominational organism) is not a self-serving social club that exists for the sake of its own members. It is a missionary sending and support system that exists to engage those who are being sanctified in active participation in God's redemptive mission. Unless a local church both gathers and sends, it perishes.

Let's take this metaphor one step further and apply it to individual church leaders, in addition to whole congregations. Missional leadership is like the electrical current that keeps a spiritual circulatory system operating. Missional leaders—whether clergy or lay—gather people together for worship, fellowship and discipleship. But they never stop there. They encourage Christ-followers to embrace an outward focus that involves them in evangelism and service. Being missional is about building up and loving one another, seeing to it that each of us uses our God-given gifts as witnesses and servants to reach out in love to those who are not yet Christ-followers.

So, start thinking and talking about your local church as a "mission force" that is sent and enabled by the Lord to make Him known in the mission field that begins next door, right in your own community.

That's the purpose of this book—to persuade you, whether you are starting a new church or leading an existing one, to be more intentionally missional. *Game Plan for Intentional Missional Ministry* is a story about the journey of one leader helping another to be purposefully on mission with God. As you identify with the characters in these pages and mull over questions like the ones they had to face, may you grow in anticipating a mighty work of God taking place right where you live and work as well.

The Wesleyan Church—the "home team" for which Tim Roehl and I play—invests heavily in four essential areas to equip local church leaders and teams with skills and spiritually strategic resources they need for developing their own game plans: assessing, coaching, training and networking. We call these our action model (A*C*T*N) for healthy church multiplication. *Game Plan* is written with this "big picture" approach always operating in the background.

Assessing leaders and churches enables them to develop greater self-awareness and confidence about where they best fit and flourish in their ministry context. Your church's missional ministry game plan needs to uncover and utilize intentional tools for evaluating...

- *Leaders*—including planters, pastors and local church ministry teams in regard to areas such as their calling, competencies, gifts, talents, personal and collective strengths and work styles;
- *Churches*—so they can develop ongoing processes for missional health and fruitfulness (see an example at *www.churchhealthprofile.com*);

- *Communities*—so congregations can design a specific "game plan" to bring Jesus to their own, unique mission field.

Coaching is a primary way to come alongside leaders in new and existing churches through a relationship and process that enables and empowers them to discover where God is working in their lives and ministries, discern opportunities and develop action steps to see God's agenda become reality. The Wesleyan Coaching Network (*www.wesleyan.org/ecg/wcn*) is a support system for creating a coaching culture in local churches, districts or beyond that we invite you to explore.

Training connects leaders and churches with the ideas, behaviors and skills they need for fruitful ministry in their mission fields. We blend onsite and online learning opportunities to make training as accessible and affordable for as many leaders as possible.

Networking acknowledges a need everyone has for meaningful connections and relationships with others who share a common vision and passion. We seek to encourage and equip leaders, leadership teams, local churches and judicatories to participate in the journey together through face-to-face and virtual meetings for sharing best practices, information, inspiration, prayer, coaching and new ideas.

Prepare to think through the key components of your own missional game plan as you read further. You will see coaching modeled in the conversations of our characters and we'll suggest powerful questions for you and your team to use in coaching yourselves to greater effectiveness. We will also point out additional assessment, training and networking opportunities and resources for you and your team to consider using.

More important than anything any book has to say, though, is your reliance on the Holy Spirit for guidance in designing a plan that is unique to you and your community. *Game Plan* is not written as a "one program fits all" solution. Rather, it is a pathway of practical principles you must adapt to your own context. As you prayerfully seek the Lord's wisdom and your team works together in His mighty power, we pray that you will develop your own game plan for intentional missional ministry that is spiritual, strategic and successful.

Jerry G. Pence
General Superintendent
The Wesleyan Church

Preface

My friend Jeff's voice had a note of uncertainty. "Man," he said, "I know what to do when I've got people, but not when I don't. What do I do?" Jeff had been a terrific youth pastor in a larger church, but now as a church planter in a new community, he was learning an uncomfortably common reality: Many North American church leaders know how to do church, but struggle to gather and reach people as a missionary. As his coach, I encouraged him that his feelings weren't unusual and said he needed to shift from "church leader" to "missionary." The Lord brought him to his new city on purpose. There was a mission field of people longing for God, waiting for someone like him to come and help them find Him!

"Great," Jeff said. "How do we do that?" That's the essential question. Living in a culture that has shifted dramatically in recent decades, ministry must be treated as cross-cultural missions in North America now more than ever. How to make the shift from traditional church leader to missional leader is a defining issue.

I began coaching Jeff to develop a game plan for approaching his city and church plant as a missionary. It was different than what he was used to, but as each step unfolded, Jeff could see the Lord going ahead of him, preparing the way for his team to demonstrate and bring the Good News of Jesus to others. Even before the new church officially launched, it became known by local leaders as a group that wanted to serve and bless the community. Now, several years later, hundreds have come to know Christ, the church continues to be highly regarded and they are starting ministries in new locations. Jeff made the shift to being a missional leader of a missional church.

In my own ministry journey, I've had the privilege of growing up going to a traditional church in a small town, being part of starting a church as a teenager; restarting a church in the heart of a large urban "heart of the city" setting; planting a church in a growing suburban environment; and being a denominational leader equipping new and existing churches leaders to start and strengthen churches to reach more people for Christ. I also had the joy of being a missionary based in North America, leading a team that focused on assessing, coaching and training leaders who serve in many denominations and nations across North America and around the world.

Take off our organizational labels and you'll find growing numbers of leaders united by a common passion to bring the Good News of Jesus to people and communities who don't know Him yet. The issues leaders face are universal. Until recent years, the majority of church planters and pastors were trained to focus their efforts on doing church better by trying to develop services and programs that will attract people to come to them. However, the Holy Spirit has been increasingly calling His leaders out of their church buildings and programs and out into their mission fields. The term "missional" is now a familiar term in ministry circles. We are learning to think, pray, go and act as missionaries in wonderful ways. Fueled by a passion for people and communities who don't yet know the transforming, powerful love of Jesus, and guided by the creative wisdom of the Holy Spirit, leaders are developing ministry starting with the needs and opportunities of their mission field, more than just relying on a particular method or style of doing church.

I've had the privilege of assessing, training and coaching hundreds leaders who long to bring Jesus to their world. One of the consistent areas we work on is developing a game plan to become great missionaries to their mission field. For most leaders, it requires shifts in priorities and activities that are uncomfortable at first, but later become more fruitful than they could imagine. Leading people to Christ fuels our passion and helps us overcome our obstacles!

This resource is a compilation of coaching conversations, training opportunities and ministry experiences I've had with hundreds of leaders. I've benefited from the wisdom of many leaders, some who I can acknowledge in these pages. Others I can't recognize with a "footnote" because I've forgotten where I've heard an important truth or ministry tip, but I do remember the power of the insight that was imprinted on my heart and mind.

Game Plan: Developing Intentional Missional Ministry is both a book and a resource manual. It's designed to help you develop a game plan for missional ministry that is both spiritual and strategic, whether you lead in a new or existing church. *Game Plan's* principles and practices are designed for you to adapt to your unique setting, trusting the Holy Spirit to give you the authority, anointing and wisdom to bring the Good News to your mission field. We'll help you become more intentional, missional and accountable in your ministry by highlighting biblical principles and practical ideas. Each section of this resource will include conversations between two leaders that illustrate the power of coaching and the essential issues we face as leaders. There will be practical "nuts and bolts" tools to help you discover and apply the insights and skills to your mission field. "Coach Yourself Forward" questions will guide you to your own game plan. We'll also suggest further resources that will help you go deeper. You'll be able to order most of them through the Wesleyan Publishing House online store at *www.wphonline.com* or find them on our website at *www.wesleyan.org/ecg*.

What's your game plan to bring Jesus to your mission field? We're praying with you that as you go and sow, the Lord of the Harvest will supernaturally make things grow!

Tim Roehl
Director of Church Health and Multiplication
The Wesleyan Church

The Journey Begins...

"Nice sermon, Pastor. I wish my neighbor could have heard that...he really needs it."

Al Johnson's grip was firm, his look sincere. Tom smiled back at him in return. "Thanks, Al, I appreciate it. Hope to see your neighbor here with you soon."

Al shook his head slightly as he replied, "I'm trying pastor, but he doesn't seem all that interested in church. I wish we could bring church to him so he could understand how much the Lord loves him...well, have a good day. Thanks again for a good message."

Tom continued shaking hands and greeting people, but Al's simple statement stuck to his heart. *"I wish we could bring church to him so he could understand how much the Lord loves him."* It was the same feeling he'd been having, too.

> **"I wish we could bring church to him so he could understand how much the Lord loves him..."**

It was more than a feeling, though...it was a growing longing.

Tom's church was doing all right in many ways. It had the ministries most churches have for their own families. Yet, he was also dealing with many of the same frustrations other pastors dealt with, at least according to his network of friends spread out around the country—each trying to serve Christ in their respective environment. All of them were trying to meet people's expectations in the church, and those expectations were as many and varied as people's preferences. Each, however, confessed to a growing sense of urgency about how many people were without Christ all around them. Somehow in the midst of all the "regular" tasks of church leadership there seemed to be little time for ministry out in their communities. Tom's church had lots of activity, but lacked a compelling focus. They didn't have the kind of influence for Christ that would consistently bring people to know Jesus and see real transformation of individuals, families and entire communities.

"I wish we could bring church to him..." Yes, Al had captured clearly what Tom had been thinking and praying about...not just bringing church to people, but bringing Jesus to his community. But how?

The lobby was almost empty now as people headed out to Sunday lunch. Tom's wife was finishing up a visit with one of her friends, giving him the signal that she'd soon be ready for their family to head home for their lunch waiting in the crockpot. Off to his right, Tom noticed Bill was praying with one of the newer men in their church who had started coming with Bill recently. Bill and his family were back from an overseas missionary assignment for a few months before beginning another term. Although this was Bill's home church, Tom didn't know him well because he'd begun his ministry while Bill and his family were still overseas. What Tom had heard about Bill made him want to know him better, though. In a country many considered spiritually resistant and nearly unreachable, Bill had been the catalyst to equip leaders who were planting churches and reaching people for Christ in amazing numbers. Whatever Bill was doing, it was working.

Walking toward him, Bill extended his hand with a warm smile. "Good word today, pastor," he said.

"Thanks," Tom said, smiling back. "Coming from a fellow minister, that means a lot."

"Well, we missionaries need to encourage each other all we can, with the size of the mission we've been given," returned Bill.

"Hey, you're the missionary," joked Tom. "I'm just a pastor."

Bill looked at him steadily for a moment before speaking. His tone was quiet but earnest. "We're all missionaries, friend. Whether here in my home church or over there in my adopted homeland, people's hearts are the same and the mission is still the same." He paused and smiled again. "I'd like to get together and hear more about what God's up to around here. Got time for coffee?"

Tom nodded. "Thanks, I'd love to. I want to hear more about what God's been doing through your ministry, too. How about lunch on Tuesday? I'll buy."

"Works for me. How about noon at that diner on Walnut just off Main? I love the home cooking and the prices." Pulling out their smart phones, they confirmed their plans.

Tom didn't know it then, but it was the first of a series of conversations that would forever change his own leadership journey, the ministry of his church and the mission field in their community.

1

through the Father's Eyes

Tuesday noon found Tom and Bill at the diner, greeting each other with the easy familiarity of men who share the common ground of ministry.

"I appreciate you meeting with me, Tom," said Bill. "Even though God's call has taken me a long way from here, I still pray often for my home church and for you. I've been looking forward to getting to know you better."

"I've been looking forward to getting to know you better, too," replied Tom. "What I hear about what the Lord is doing through your ministry is pretty amazing. I'd love to know more about what you've done to see those results."

Bill smiled. "I'd be glad to talk ministry, but first I want to learn more about you, your family and your ministry journey. What's your story?"

"Ok, I'll tell you my story if you'll tell me yours," Tom smiled back in return.

"Sounds good...you first." With that, Bill leaned forward slightly with a look that said, "I'm listening...what you have to say is important to me."

Tom found himself sharing his story easily as Bill listened intently, occasionally nodding and graciously asking questions that opened doors for Tom to share even more. As he related how God had worked through the experiences and people of his life, Tom sensed a deep reaffirmation of the Lord's call for him. He found himself sharing with Bill some of his greatest joys, challenges and longings to fulfill the call Christ had on his life and church, including his thoughts about bringing Jesus to their community from the previous Sunday. Even though Bill didn't say much, his ministry of listening was a powerful gift to Tom. Finally, Tom leaned back in his chair and grinned sheepishly. "Wow. I didn't intend on sharing all that! Thanks for listening."

"Glad to," replied Bill. "You've got quite a story. It sounds like Jesus has really been speaking to you in some deep ways, especially in your desire to bring His love through our church to our community. Like I said Sunday, we're all missionaries. I can tell you are on the way to overcoming some of the biggest obstacles I've had to overcome in my ministry."

"Thanks," Tom said. "I think I'm beginning to understand what you mean about being a missionary a bit better. You said you had to overcome some big obstacles. What were they?"

"Before I tell you about them, could I share part of my story?" Bill replied. "I had an experience that forever changed some things for me, especially how I view my mission."

Now Tom leaned forward to listen. "Please," he said. "Tell me more."

Bill looked down for a moment, and when he looked up again it was as if he was looking back in time, reliving a signature event. "Well," he said, "It happened a number of years ago when my brother, Dad and I were deer hunting. I still regard that day as one of the most frightening times in my life. We were eleven miles out in the middle of nowhere—way beyond any paved roads, gravel roads, and even the muddy, rutted, logging roads in that part of the forest where we hunted every fall. Our deer stands were scattered out in those deep woods, along faint game trails in the midst of birch, pine and maple trees, carpeted with dense, bushy undergrowth. The forest went for miles. Make a wrong turn and a man could be lost for a long time. It was a mistake that could have deadly consequences."

"One cold day, my brother forgot his way as evening descended though. I heard Randy call to me from the increasing darkness, a note of uncertainty in his voice—'Bill?' I called back to him, urgency in mine: 'Randy, I'm over here!' Walking toward his voice, we called to each other for a long time, until he saw my waving flashlight and we found each other. He was exhausted by trying to find his way in the dark, boggy underbrush. I practically carried him, our rifles and our backpacks out of the woods to our hunting cabin, where our father waited anxiously. I'll never forget Dad calling across the dark meadow as we came toward him— "Are there one or two?" I called back, 'We're both here!' Later, after Randy collapsed exhausted into bed, my Dad said to me, 'I'm sure glad you went back in after him.' My response without even thinking was, 'I wasn't coming back without him.'"

Bill stopped and looked at Tom. His moist eyes and the expression on Bill's face were evidence of how deeply the experience still affected him.

"Tom, the words 'lost' and 'found' have never been the same to me since. As I've thought about that night, I realized that life got very simple when my brother's life was at stake. My mission became singularly

"Life got very simple when my brother's life was at stake. My mission became singularly clear."

clear. Nothing else mattered but finding my brother and bringing him home safely. Now, I really understand what Jesus meant when He said He came to seek and save the lost. Everything has been different since, especially in how I view ministry."

The two men sat silently in the significance of what Bill had shared. As they did, the Spirit of God spoke to Tom, igniting passion for lost people deep within him, sharpening his sense of call into a singular mission.

Bill spoke quietly again. "I can tell you more of my story and our ministry, but everything I am and do comes from what the Lord imprinted on my heart that night about seeking the lost. That one central passion defines and fuels my mission. That's what helped me overcome those obstacles I talked about before."

Tom nodded in understanding. "Thank you. What you shared is clarifying some things for me, too. I'm afraid I've been too scattered and vague about my sense of mission. It shows in our church, too. I haven't had the urgency about lost people that I need. The Lord and I have some things to work through about that. What were the obstacles you mentioned?"

"There were two main obstacles," Bill said. "First, I realized that I was more in love with a particular model of ministry, than I was burdened for the lost people in my mission field. Second, I knew how to 'do church,' but I didn't know how to think and act as a missionary. I'd allowed myself to live with those barriers, somehow considering them acceptable excuses for 'church as usual' ministry. But when the Lord gave me a holy urgency for lost people, I couldn't let them hinder me anymore. I had to change the way I approached ministry. It wasn't easy, but it's been worth it."

Main barriers to missional ministry:

1. **Leaders who are more in love with a model than their mission field.**

2. **Leaders who know how to "do church" but don't know how to be a missionary to their community.**

"You're not the only one with those obstacles," Tom admitted. "That's my current reality. But how can I overcome them? I want that holy urgency you talked about. I want to see a continual stream of lost people coming to Christ. I want to see the Lord use our church to see real transformation in our community…our mission field." He looked at Bill, his face a mix of desperation and determination. "Would you be willing to walk with me…help me? I've been stuck too long…too many people are lost without Jesus."

"Tom," Bill said, "It would be an honor. If you want, we can meet regularly and see how you can become the lead missionary of a church full of missionaries to our community."

"Thanks, Bill…I'd like that." The two set up a time to meet later that week at a local coffee shop before quietly praying together for each other, those around them in the diner, their church and their mission field.

"Holy urgency…lost people." The words echoed in Tom's spirit long afterwards. They became the plea of his heart, as he and Jesus talked long into the night.

Our Singular Aspiration…His Mission

Sometimes it takes a dramatically defining experience to focus life on what matters most. The defining event of all human history was when Jesus left His home in heaven and went on a rescue mission compelled by His love. Seeking us when we were lost and captive, He literally laid down His life so we could be redeemed, reconciled and restored to a right relationship to our Father. It was His singular mission.

God's church is strongest when we focus on the singular mission we've been given. Jesus described His redemptive mission in a number of ways. Read these verses and capture your insights about the scope of His mission.

"Then he added, "Now go and learn the meaning of this Scripture: 'I want you to show mercy, not offer sacrifices.' For I have come to call not those who think they are righteous, but those who know they are sinners." (Matthew 9:13 NLT)

"The Son of Man came not to be served but to serve others and to give His life as a ransom for many." (Mark 10:45 NIV)

"The Spirit of the Lord is on me, because he has anointed me to proclaim good news to the poor. He has sent me to proclaim freedom for the prisoners and recovery of sight for the blind, to set the oppressed free, [19] *to proclaim the year of the Lord's favor." (Luke 4:18-19 NIV)*

"The Son of Man has come to seek and save the lost..." (Luke 19:10 NIV)

"For God loved the world so much that he gave his one and only Son, so that everyone who believes in him will not perish but have eternal life. God sent his Son into the world not to judge the world, but to save the world through him." (John 3:16-17, NLT)

"The thief comes only to steal and destroy, but I have come to give them life, and have it abundantly." (John 10:10, ESV)

"Then Jesus came to them and said, "All authority in heaven and on earth has been given to Me. Therefore go and make disciples of all nations, baptizing them in the name of the Father and of the Son and of the Holy Spirit, and teaching them to obey everything I have commanded you. And surely I am with you always, to the very end of the age." (Matthew 28:18-20 NIV)

As God's Church, there are many things we can do that are good, but everything must flow from and contribute to the singular mission He's given us: go into our world like He did and make disciples.

- When we see our world as our Father does and our hearts are broken by what breaks our Father's heart...
- When our hearts are cleansed and filled by holy love and the Holy Spirit leads us...
- When we see the wonder and joy of lives and communities being transformed by Jesus...
- Then we experience the fullness of our Father's love and join Him willingly in His redemptive mission.

COACH YOURSELF FORWARD

1. What "defining events" have influenced your heart for lost people?
2. What does the reality of "lost" and "found" mean to you?
3. What keeps you focused and fueled on God's mission?
4. What did you learn from the Scripture verses where Jesus described His mission that will influence your church's attitude toward His mission in your community?
5. How could you help your church develop God's heart for lost people?
6. What are the consequences of not making God's redemptive mission a top priority of your ministry?
7. Begin to brainstorm some ways you and your church could join Jesus on His redemptive mission. What ideas come to you at this point?

When they met again, Tom was eager to share the work that Jesus had been doing in his heart to give him a holy urgency for lost people. "Bill," he said, "what the Lord's been doing in me has been unsettling, uncomfortable and deep. I can't live the same way or do church the same way anymore. Our denomination's mission is to fulfill the Great Commission in the Spirit of the Great Commandment. The Great Commission has too often an omission for our church and me. Not any more. Now it's going to be primary in all we do. Now when I'm out among people, I find myself wondering how many of them are lost and without Christ...and what it's going to take to reach them. The Lord has ignited something in me. I want to keep that fire burning bright and see my whole church lit up, too."

Bill nodded in understanding affirmation. "You're right...being focused on the harvest and fueled by holy love go hand in glove. You can't have one without the other. I'm glad to hear how you've been thinking differently about the Great Commission. The Lord's also helped me understand some things about the Great Commission that have impacted my view of ministry."

"What did you learn that made such a difference?" Tom asked. "We've heard the words of the Great Commission so often that they've become too familiar and easy to skip over."

"There were a few simple truths that transformed my understanding of the Great Commission," Bill said, "But first let me ask you...what's the most important part of the Great Commission to you?"

Tom thought for a moment. "Well," he replied. "The heart of the Great Commission for me is making disciples."

"Good," nodded Bill. "That's the heart of our mission...everything we do must be about making disciples. What changed for me was my attitude about *how* I was to do that."

"What do you mean?"

"I had been approaching ministry, especially as a missionary, with some assumptions that held me back. My biggest hindrance was that I made God too small and my obstacles too big. I approached ministry from a posture of weakness...that the cultural barriers and spiritual opposition from our enemy were too much to overcome. I expected to lose and so I held back and played it safe. That made it easier to focus on ministry inside the church, instead of going on mission outside our doors."

"Like the ten spies in Numbers 13 who scouted out the land God promised His people, but reported that the giants there were so big that the spies looked like grasshoppers?" Tom asked.

"Exactly," nodded Bill. "We are truly in a battle for souls. If we believe we're weak and helpless, we lose the battle before we ever start. The ten spies had that attitude, and their negative influence caused God's people to wander around for a long time, instead of confidently pursuing the mission God gave them."

"All authority in heaven and earth have been given to Me… therefore, go… I am with you always…"

"Sounds like too many churches today," Tom shook his head sadly. "Including mine."

"That's where a holy urgency for lost people made such a difference for me," said Bill. "Like Scripture says in 2 Corinthians 5:14, I became compelled by the love of Christ, but had to change my attitude of weakness that held me back. One day, while reading the Great Commission passage, some words lit up like I was seeing them for the first time. The truth of those words changed my attitude."

"What were they?" Tom leaned forward, listening intently.

"All authority in heaven and earth have been given to Me…therefore, go…I am with you always…" Bill said, his face shining. "There it was! Jesus has all authority. He's already won the victory. He's already gone ahead of me, and He is sending me with His authority! He's with me! When I understood the spiritual authority we have in Jesus, my attitude changed. I knew there were still battles to fight and obstacles to overcome, but now I realized that I could pray and act from a position of victory,

not defeat. For me, understanding spiritual authority has now become the activating power for Great Commission ministry. It was a dimension of the Spirit-filled life I had not really appreciated before. "

Bill paused and looked at Tom. "What does spiritual authority look like in your life and ministry?"

Tom was silent, the look on his face signaling that the question had touched something unexpected and deep in him. Bill just waited. Finally, Tom replied, "That's a really good question. I really haven't given the issue as much attention as I should have. The way you describe it as the key to the Great Commission really makes sense. Now that the Lord has given me a passion and mission to focus on reaching lost people so they become disciples, how do I understand and apply spiritual authority with the attitude you described?

Bill grinned in return. "Good question! Would you like to focus on that issue for the rest of our conversation today?"

Tom nodded. "Absolutely."

With that focus, their conversation continued, with Bill asking questions that helped Tom to clarify his understanding of spiritual authority. They looked at passages in Scripture, talked about the theological issues involved, and identified some concerns and discoveries about the nature of spiritual authority. Bill invited Tom to generate some options about how he could grow in his understanding of spiritual authority and begin applying those truths to his life and ministry.

Before they left, Tom had developed some clear action steps involving further Bible study, resources to read, and conversations he would have with others about understanding and activating spiritual authority as leaders and as a church. Tom found himself scribbling discoveries and action steps on a napkin. There was a look of hope in his eyes. This conversation had taken him from discovering a need in his life to developing specific steps to move him forward to address that need!

Bill tapped the notes on the napkin with a smile. "The game plan you've come up with looks really good, Tom," said Bill. "Good job!"

Tom smiled back in return. "Back at you! Whatever you just did sure helped me...thank you!"

"I've had the benefit of having some good coaching, and it's really helped me. Coaching was so powerful for me that I decided to learn how to coach others, too. I was using coaching skills in our conversation. I'm glad you found what we did helpful."

"It sure was...keep doing it!" Tom said. "And...could you help me learn how to do that for others? I think these skills will really help me equip my leaders better. When can we meet again?"

"I like the way you're thinking!" Bill said. "Let's set a time for our next visit...and keep me updated on your progress. How about praying for each other before we head out into the rest of our day?"

The two men prayed, shook hands and headed for their cars. As he drove home, Tom reflected on the discoveries and impact his conversations with Bill were making on him. Not only had the Lord given him clarity and passion about a singular sense of mission, Tom felt his attitude and approach to becoming a Great Commission leader had shifted powerfully. As he silently gave thanks, he felt the Holy Spirit whisper to him, "There's more coming, son. I'm with you."

"More, Lord...more, please." As Tom's spirit and the Spirit of God continued that conversation, the space in his car became sacred ground.

His Spiritual Authority—Our Power

Remember this: it is the Lord of the Harvest who sends us! We go commissioned by the King of the Universe to carry out His purposes, authorized with His power. Many Christians look around them and bemoan how bad things are "out there." When we focus our attention on the disintegration of morality in our society, hostility toward Jesus in cultural media and the visibly increasing activity of Satan, it is easy to be fearful and retreat to the relative safety of hiding behind the walls of our churches and Christian environments. Too often God's people see themselves as weak and unable to engage the world redemptively because people in our culture aren't interested and the spiritual resistance is too strong.

That's a lie! Our focus is in the wrong place. We're listening to the wrong voices. Step back...take another look. Listen again to the longings of people around you. Listen to another Voice and you'll see a different view that energizes you with courage and power.

Here's something most people miss when talking about the Great Commission: We focus on the task we've been given, instead of on the resources we have to accomplish the mission. Think of "commission" as "co-mission." We are on mission *with* Jesus. He starts by reminding us that all authority is His. We have the power of the Holy Spirit filling us and activating His power. That's the oft-forgotten secret of the Great Commission!

The issue of spiritual authority generates much discussion among God's people. Some theological viewpoints tend to ignore it all together, while others carry it to an unbiblical extreme. Because understanding spiritual authority can be controversial, many leaders tend to shy away from it. We can't afford to do that! Our attitude and approach toward applying spiritual authority in our ministries is essential to carrying out the Lord's redemptive mission. Become a student of this issue using John Wesley's quadrilateral approach.

Learn from Scripture, tradition and history, reason and experience. This is a vital part of our "on the job training" for missional ministry!

Jesus has all authority. The battle's already won. Victory is already secure. Our enemy is a defeated foe. Christ has already gone ahead of us. He's given His power and authority to use wherever He sends us. We can confidently go with Jesus using the supernatural resources He provides!

Read these passages from Scripture. What do they teach you about spiritual authority?

"Jesus now called the Twelve and gave them authority and power to deal with all the demons and cure diseases. He commissioned them to preach the news of God's kingdom and heal the sick. He said, 'Don't load yourselves up with equipment. Keep it simple; you are the equipment…. Commissioned, they began their circuit of the villages, preaching the Good News and healing the sick…'" (Luke 9:1-3, 6 MSG)

"…I will build My church, a church so expansive with energy that not even the gates of hell will be able to keep it out. And that's not all. I will give you the keys of the kingdom of heaven. You will have complete and free access to God's kingdom, keys to open any and every door: whatever you bind on earth will be bound in heaven, and whatever you loose on earth will be loosed in heaven." (Matthew 16:18-19, MSG)

"Then Jesus came to them and said, "All authority in heaven and on earth has been given to me. Therefore go and make disciples of all nations, baptizing them in the name of the Father and of the Son and of the Holy Spirit, and teaching them to obey everything I have commanded you. I'll be with you as you do this, day after day after day, right up to the end of the age." (Matthew 28:18-20 NIV)

"For this reason, ever since I heard about your faith in the Lord Jesus and your love for all God's people, I have not stopped

giving thanks for you, remembering you in my prayers. I keep asking that the God of our Lord Jesus Christ, the glorious Father, may give you the Spirit of wisdom and revelation, so that you may know him better. I pray that the eyes of your heart may be enlightened in order that you may know the hope to which he has called you, the riches of his glorious inheritance in his holy people, and his incomparably great power for us who believe. That power is the same as the mighty strength he exerted when he raised Christ from the dead and seated him at his right hand in the heavenly realms, far above all rule and authority, power and dominion, and every name that is invoked, not only in the present age but also in the one to come. And God placed all things under his feet and appointed him to be head over everything for the church, which is his body, the fullness of him who fills everything in every way." (Ephesians 1:15-23 NIV)

"Finally, be strong in the Lord and in his mighty power. Put on the full armor of God, so that you can take your stand against the devil's schemes. For our struggle is not against flesh and blood, but against the rulers, against the authorities, against the powers of this dark world and against the spiritual forces of evil in the heavenly realms. Therefore put on the full armor of God, so that when the day of evil comes, you may be able to stand your ground, and after you have done everything, to stand. Stand firm then, with the belt of truth buckled around your waist, with the breastplate of righteousness in place, and with your feet fitted with the readiness that comes from the gospel of peace. In addition to all this, take up the shield of faith, with which you can extinguish all the flaming arrows of the evil one. Take the helmet of salvation and the sword of the Spirit, which is the word of God. And pray in the Spirit on all occasions with all kinds of prayers and requests. With this in mind, be alert and always keep on praying for all the Lord's people. Pray also for me, that whenever I speak, words may be given me so that I will fearlessly make known the mystery of the gospel, for which I am an ambassador

*in chains. Pray that I may declare it fearlessly, as I should."
(Ephesians 6:10-20 NIV)*

*"Therefore God exalted him to the highest place and gave him
the name that is above every name, that at the name of Jesus
every knee should bow, in heaven and on earth and under the
earth, and every tongue acknowledge that Jesus Christ is Lord, to
the glory of God the Father." (Philippians 2:9-11 NIV)*

COACH YOURSELF FORWARD

1. How does Bill and Tom's conversation about the Great
   Commission influence your understanding of it?
2. What's your current understanding of spiritual authority?
   Study the Scripture passages we've listed. What insights do
   you gain about Jesus' victory, the nature of spiritual
   authority and your ministry?
3. In what ways can you learn about spiritual authority using
   Wesley's quadrilateral principles—learning from Scripture,
   tradition, reason and experience?
4. In what ways are you applying spiritual authority in your
   ministry?
5. What teaching or training have you done about spiritual
   authority with your ministry teams?
6. How can you activate and increase spiritual authority in your
   ministry?
7. How big is your God?

Our Mission Field—They're Waiting

Not only do we need to have God's viewpoint as we are sent on His
mission with His authority, we also need to have an energizing
perspective about our mission field. Scripture helps us "see" the
reality of eternity in ways that haunt us and motivate us to action. In

the light of eternity and the certainty of Christ's return, we are motivated with holy urgency!

> "Summer is over, the harvest is past...and we are not saved." (Jeremiah 8:20 NIV)

> "Multitudes, multitudes in the valley of decision! For the day of the Lord is near in the valley of decision." (Joel 3:14 NIV)

> "But the exact day and hour? No one knows that, not even heaven's angels, not even the Son. Only the Father. So keep a sharp lookout, for you don't know the timetable. It's like a man who takes a trip, leaving home and putting his servants in charge, each assigned a task, and commanding the gatekeeper to stand watch. So, stay at your post, watching. You have no idea when the homeowner is returning, whether evening, midnight, cockcrow, or morning. You don't want him showing up unannounced, with you asleep on the job. I say it to you, and I'm saying it to all: Stay at your post. Keep watch." (Mark 13:32-37 MSG)

Authors Tom Clegg (*Missing in America*) and Dave Olson (*The American Church in Crisis*) have captured some statistics that make us look at our mission field in North America in some unsettling ways. Based on their findings, in the next twenty-four hours across North America,

- *11,350 babies will be born and 6,663 people will die*
- *6,110 couples will get married and 3,110 will divorce*
- *3,242 children will be aborted and there will be 4,106 illegitimate births*
- *87 will commit suicide, 36 will die from AIDS, 49 will be murdered and there will be 43 alcohol-related deaths*
- *12, 267 children under 13 will take their first drink*
- *2,948 children under 13 will have sex for the first time*
- *1,312 drop-outs and 4,400 teens will start smoking*
- *28,206 will be arrested—4,274 for drug-related offenses*

- *3,396 will declare bankruptcy*
- *63,288 will go on food stamps*
- *68,493 people will be treated for depression*
- *411 will convert to Islam*
- *827 will become Mormons*
- *10 churches will close their doors permanently*

Thousands will die without knowing the love of Christ in a "Valley of Decision" called North America. Consider these facts about the North American mission field:

Fact #1—North America is the only continent where Christianity is *not* growing.

Fact #2—The decline in Christianity has been going on for nearly fifty years...there are now over 280 *million* unchurched people in the United States and Canada.

Fact #3—In the past 15 years, churches in the USA have spent 500 *billion* dollars on buildings and programs...with *no* appreciable growth.

Fact #4—On any given Sunday, about 80% of people are not attending any place of worship and 80% of churches are plateaued or in decline.

Fact #5—Over half of all churches in America did not add *one* new member through conversion last year.

Fact #6—About 10 churches per day are closing their doors. New churches are 11 times more effective reaching people for Christ than existing churches! We need nearly 3,000 more churches per year more than we are planting now just to keep up with population growth in our country.

Fact #7—North America is the largest English speaking mission field in the world.

Fact #8—Far too many churched people believe and behave identically to their unchurched counterparts.

Fact #9—Conversions to other religions and dropouts from Christianity are escalating. It is estimated that 53,000 people leave churches every week and never come back. (*Exit Interviews,* George Hendricks)

Fact #10—No matter how you do the math, current conversion rates still point to one horrible conclusion: *lost people lose.*

When you see statistics like these, it can appear that our mission field is resistant. However, when we take a deeper look, we find that people are much more ready and receptive than we think. People are waiting for us to come. Thom

> **Our mission field is ripe…ready…and more receptive than we realize! People are waiting for us to come.**

Rainer, in his book "*The Unchurched Next Door*" offers insights into the attitudes of people that are often different than we think. Here's a quick summary of some of Rainer's discoveries:

1. Most unchurched people prefer to attend church on Sunday morning, if they attend.
2. Females are most likely to be either the most receptive or antagonistic toward the gospel.
3. Most unchurched people feel guilty about not attending church.
4. 82% of unchurched people are at least "somewhat likely" to attend church if they are invited. Yet, only 21% of active church attenders invite anyone to church in a given year… and only 2% of Christians invite an unchurched person to attend church with them!
5. Very few unchurched people have had someone share with them how to become a Christian…and Christians have not been very influential in their lives.
6. Most unchurched people have positive views of pastors and the church.
7. Some types of "cold calls" are effective, but many aren't. The Lord may nudge us to engage a stranger in a spiritual

conversation, but most of the time we should build relationships with people in order to share Jesus with them.

8. Unchurched people would like to develop a real and sincere relationship with a Christian.

9. The attitudes of unchurched people are not correlated to geography, ethnicity or gender.

10. Many unchurched people are far more concerned about the spiritual wellbeing of their kids than themselves.

Not only are people much more receptive spiritually than we give them credit for, but many are waiting for us to come to them, listen to them, care for them and share what Jesus has done for us and what He can do for them, too! Multitudes hang in the balance. What should our response be to this vast mission field at our door? As John Wesley said to his corps of lay ministers: *"You have nothing to do but save souls; therefore spend and be spent in this work; and go always not only to those who desire you, but to those who need you most."*

COACH YOURSELF FORWARD

1. What verses in Scripture "haunt" and motivate you to reach lost people?

2. Why is it so hard to see our nation as a mission field?

3. What stood out to you on our 24-hour journey looking at "mission field North America"?

4. Personalize the statistics we looked at. Who do you know that represents some of those stats? What are their names? What happens when "numbers become names"?

5. How did Thom Rainer's discoveries about the attitudes of unchurched people affect you?

6. How could you begin to apply what you learned from Rainer's study in your relationships?

7. Summarize what you've learned about joining Jesus on His redemptive mission in the mission field in your area.

FURTHER RESOURCES

The Unchurched Next Door by Thom Rainer (Zondervan, 2008)

Surprising Insights from the Previously Unchurched by Thom Rainer (Zondervan, 2008)

Lost in America by Tom Clegg (Group Publishing, 2001)

Missing in America by Tom Clegg (Group Publishing, 2007)

The American Church in Crisis by David Olson (Zondervan, 2008)

Nothing to Do But Save Souls by Robert Coleman (Francis Asbury Press, 2006)

2

"Shifting"

to Align with the Father's Purposes

The smell of fresh coffee filled the air as Tom and Bill placed their orders at the local coffee shop.

"I've been looking forward to this visit," said Tom. "I've been sharing with some fellow pastors around town and some of my ministry buddies around the country what the Lord's been doing in me. Troy is planting a church in the heart of the city in a large urban setting. Chris pastors a church in a rural area where the church has been there a long time. Both the population of the area and the church are struggling with decline. Sue is on staff at a large suburban church. We are all in very different ministry environments, but we keep up with each other online and by phone. The interesting thing for me is that the Lord has been talking to them about some of the same things! It's like the Holy Spirit has us on the same learning journey together."

Bill smiled. "It's interesting how the Spirit does that, isn't it? I've learned that when He's saying the same thing to different people in different places, I'd better pay close attention. Sounds like He's up to something that's bigger than just you and me."

Tom nodded in agreement. "I think you're right. Since we've been meeting, some things are really becoming clear for me. At the same time, it seems like I've got more questions than ever. My sense of call and mission are sharper than they've been for a long time. I feel like I'm closer to the Lord and seeing my world through His eyes in fresh ways. What I've been learning about my identity in Christ and spiritual authority has been really powerful. But if I'm going to live out His call, I can tell that I'm going to have to shift some things both in what I think and what I do. How can I be so clear and so confused at the same time?"

Bill nodded. "I can relate. The Lord led me through a very similar process. Once He gripped me with His heart for lost people, He had to help me get aligned with His purposes. Believe me, I had a lot of things that needed realignment! It started while I was still in ministry here in North America, but really became obvious when I became a missionary to another culture. As the Lord helped me make some important shifts, it really helped me overcome the barriers I mentioned to you. I had focused primarily on a particular model of doing church as a typical church leader, instead of making it first about Jesus and the people He sent me to reach."

"What were the shifts the Lord helped you make?" Tom asked.

"There were many overall, but the more I've thought about it, things really boiled down to some very simple issues I had to put in right priority in order to align myself with the Father's purposes. I heard three words from Alan Hirsh that helped clarify and simplify some essential issues for me." Bill pulled out his notepad and wrote three words from left to right—

Christology... Missiology... Ecclesiology

"It didn't take me long to realize I had these out of order."

"How so?" Tom asked curiously.

"Basically, I had them backwards. I started by determining what kind of church I wanted. I thought I was supposed to come up with a vision, start my ministry and then get people to come to my church. I hate to admit it, but I was really more in love with my vision and the kind of church I wanted than the Lord of the Church! On top of that, I realize now that I'd given little thought to whether the kind of church I wanted was what the people in my mission field needed. It didn't take me long to realize that my ideal church and the church that would make Jesus real to the people in my mission field where not very compatible. Some of the very things I was most enamored with about how I wanted to do church were actually hindering people from coming to Christ! It was a painful lesson to learn."

"What did you do?" Tom asked.

Bill smiled ruefully. "I wish I could tell you that I easily and willingly made the adjustments when I realized my priorities were messed up. After all, it was *my* vision for *my* church! I'm grateful for how patient and merciful Jesus was with me. He had to bring me to a fresh place of surrender…I had to lay down my vision and remember that it was *His* church. Even more, it was all about *Him* and His Kingdom." Bill pointed to the words on the paper. I had "ecclesiology"—my idea of church—first. After giving my church back to Jesus, He now became first." He pointed to the word "Christology" on the paper. "Praying 'Thy Kingdom come…Thy will be done…' now had new meaning to me."

Tom paused for a moment, taking a long sip of coffee. "I think you've been reading my mail. What you're describing hits close to home. There's another dimension, though. Not only am I dealing with my personal preferences, there are also the expectations and preferences of my people. Everyone has their own idea of what church should be according to their wants."

Bill chuckled. "Some things are universal, aren't they? That's where the Lord pointed out to me one more defining issue that had to be in proper alignment." He pointed to the world "missiology" on the paper. "I now had Jesus as my top priority, but I still had to discern what kind of church He wanted me to lead. That's where learning how to think and act as a missionary became so important. In order to know what kind of church the Lord wanted, not only did I need to understand how He'd wired and gifted me to lead, I also had to learn the needs of the people He'd called me to reach. I knew there were some biblical essentials every church needs—I call them my 'Five E's for Every Church.' But we had to adapt those essentials to connect to the culture we ministered in. The mission field shapes the style of church. Someone once told me that the church must be more concerned about reaching the lost than losing the reached.

> **The church must be more concerned about reaching the lost than losing the reached.**

When I determined that my church had to be designed around the priority of reaching lost people, things came into proper alignment for me… Christology, Missiology, Ecclesiology. Three simple words in the right priority made all the difference."

Tom nodded thoughtfully. "I get it…that makes real sense to me. I want to talk more about that, but you've made me curious. What are your 'Five E's for Every Church'?"

Bill pulled out another sheet of paper and began to write. "These are just my way of describing what so many others have written about…but the issue for me now is *how* we should shape these essentials according to the needs and opportunities of our mission field." Bill finished writing and turned the paper around so Tom could read it:

Five E's for Every Church

Exalt God through worship
Edify people to wholeness
Equip people for the work of ministry
Evangelize through our witness
Extend His Kingdom to our world

Tom nodded as he read. "Those are pretty common thoughts, all right. What isn't common is putting missiology as a key influence for ecclesiology. Your three words in that priority raise a lot more questions for me about the different shifts I'll need to make in my own thinking…and in our church's ministries. Could we make that our focus for the rest of the conversation? I'm enjoying the way you are coaching me."

"Sure," Bill said. "You set the agenda and we'll get you to some action steps. As a coach, I have a game plan to walk through with you… and if I do it well, you'll leave with a game plan you've discovered and developed for yourself."

"Do you mind sharing with me what your coaching game plan is?" Tom asked, as he smiled playfully. "Or is it a secret for only a select few?"

Bill returned Tom's tease with a grin. "No secrets, no code words, no special handshake. In fact, my game plan is pretty simple. As a coach, my goal is to see people become more like Jesus and join Him on His redemptive mission to grow His Kingdom. Coaches help people grow by asking good questions that lead to discovery. That's better than just me giving my advice. In fact, my coaching game plan is based on that word—G-R-O-W."

Taking another sheet of paper, he wrote the letters G-R-O-W vertically. "Here's the path we'll walk.

G is our Goal. That's our focus and determines the result you want to get from our conversation.

R is for Reality. We have to paint a picture of what is really going on that is influencing our situation.

O is for Options. We ask the Holy Spirit to help us generate possibilities to accomplish our goal.

W is for Will … as in what "will" you do. This is where we clarify action steps so that you can move forward with your game plan."

Tom's eyes lit up with discovery. "I can see how you've been doing that with me. It sure helps. So, I've identified the goal. Let's keep going."

Bill smiled. "Sounds good. Glad we're at a place that gives us free refills! This is going to be a fun conversation."

Coffee drinking, questions, animated conversation and discovery continued. When they were finished, Tom had written a list of biblical passages he wanted to study for further insights about God's missional priorities. Tom and Bill brainstormed a number of "shifts" that needed to be made for him to become a missional leader in a changing culture. They also made a list of different people in Tom's church that he would begin to converse with about what the Lord was doing in his heart.

Tom leaned back in his chair with the look of someone enjoying a job well done. "Thanks, Bill," Tom said. "You did a good job with your game plan as a coach. Now I have a game plan to work on in the coming days. When can we get together again? Let's put something on the calendar now."

Bill pulled out his smart phone. "I'll be on the road for the next few weeks, visiting other churches. How does the 25th look for you?"

Tom confirmed the date and time. "Got it—and next time I'm buying the coffee."

Form Missional Priorities

Although ministry can appear very complex, at the heart of things are some clear issues that need to be aligned with our Father's purposes. As my friend Dave DeVries, a veteran missionary, coach and church planting trainer, observes, "It's about alignment, not assignment; disciples, not decisions; and being church, more than doing church."

Let's revisit the essential issues Bill identified that formed his missional priorities. As you develop your ministry strategy, keep this supernatural sequence of priorities in mind:

Christology. It's always about Jesus and His Kingdom first and foremost...not about us, our church, affiliation or style. Start by focusing on Who sends us. We are chosen by, committed to and commissioned with authority by Jesus.

Missiology. We join Jesus on His redemptive mission by discerning and developing a profile of our mission field. We want to fit and flourish where God has sent us, and relate effectively and redemptively to people there. Key missional questions we need to ask include: Who has Jesus sent us to reach? How can we translate the Good News to these people so they can understand, respond and become disciples of Jesus?

Ecclesiology. We discern and develop the form of "church" needed to bring Christ to our mission field! A key missional question is, "What *could* church look like to bring Jesus to this culture?"

The missional process can be described in several other ways:

- "Sent...Student...Servant...Storyteller."

- "Discerning listening, divine appointments, determining needs, developing ministries, deploying teams."

- "Leaving our own, living among, listening to, loving redemptively, linking to community."

The principles of Scripture give us the keys to developing the unique missional game plan for your mission field. Although the principles are woven throughout the whole Bible, there are some places that are especially helpful for us to gain insights for missional ministry. Let's highlight a few passages briefly (see Appendix B for fuller outlines based on these passages).

Joshua: God's Field Guide to Take the Promised Land

The book of Joshua is still used by military leaders as a great field manual. It is also a powerful guide for spiritual warriors today. Throughout Joshua you'll find how God sanctified and shaped His leaders, gave them strategies for engaging their adversaries and supernaturally brought victory.

Numbers 13: Spy Out the Land

As you seek God's wisdom for your ministry, remember these key lessons from Numbers 13:

1. Like Moses did with the 12 spies, it is important to "spy out the land" before you go in. This is called spiritual surveying or mapping.
2. Like the 12 spies, you need to be able to identify the strongholds of the enemy that keep people captive.
3. Like Joshua and Caleb, you must also identify the opportunities and assets of the land and "redemptive gifts" Jesus wants to release to set people free.
4. Remember, God is greater than the enemy! It's His power and authority that make the difference!

Acts: God's Multiplication Manual

Apostles and disciples in the early church were the first to live out Great Commission strategies with the supernatural anointing and authority of the Holy Spirit. The combination of sanctified love from a pure heart, spiritual authority to defeat Satan and supernatural power for miracles made biblical multiplication an amazing reality. Disciples today still look to Acts for the principles that make multiplication possible.

Luke 9 and 10: Jesus' Strategy for Reaching New Communities

Luke 9 and 10 describe how Jesus commissioned His team and sent them ahead of Him to prepare the way for His arrival. The integration of spiritual authority with gracious incarnational and proclamational ministry that we find in Luke is a pattern for missional ministry strategizing today.

Make Missional Shifts

"Missional" means we approach ministry as missionaries who are sent by God and blessed by Him to be a blessing to others! This commission is as old as the Lord's covenant with Abraham in Genesis 12. In our generation, it means personally and simultaneously expressing the Great Commandment (Matthew 22:36-40) and the Great Commission (Matthew 28:18-20).

Reggie McNeal, in his book *Missional Renaissance*, suggests three major shifts we must make:

1. From inward to outward—focusing on the lost more than the already converted.
2. From doing programs to developing people—focusing on equipping disciples to be disciple-makers.
3. From church to Kingdom—focusing on the big picture of what God is doing, not just our specific church.

In other words, we need to learn the distinction between missional and attractional approaches to ministry. The idea of becoming more missional is growing for many leaders. Many churches have had more of an attractional approach. They consciously or unconsciously expect people to come to them so they can tell them about Jesus. When people do come, though, attractional churches must figure out how to translate God's Good News, so that it is understandable for unchurched people. More and more people in our culture don't know God and aren't familiar with church language and practices. As Colossians 4:2-6 reminds us, it is our responsibility and privilege to take the mystery out of knowing God. It is our responsibility to translate the Good News so others can understand. Missional leaders realize that it should not be the unchurched person's burden to have to interpret what we are saying! Missional and attractional approaches to ministry are both important. It's not either/or but both/and. Here's a brief comparison of the two approaches.

Shifts that are affecting missional ministry in our culture...

Generational	Builder/Boomer	to	Buster/Beginner
Cultural	Modern	to	Post modern & Premodern
Philosophical	Organizational	to	Organic/relational
Method	Attractional	to	Missional/"Missionally attractive"
Supported	Fully funded	to	Bi-vocational
Organizational	Denomination/ District centered	to	Parent/Multi-site
Scope	Local	to	Glocal
Planting Strategy	Attract a crowd... start a church	to	Engage community...do ministry...start church
Posture	Apologist Proclamational Head first/word	to	Missiologist Incarnational Heart first/worship/ experience
Training	Content centered	to	Context centered

There has been lots of discussion about the words "attractional" and "missional." We need to be both...but be missional first! When we go (missional), we earn the right to be heard. When we expect people to come to us (attractional), we must work hard to translate timeless truth in timely ways...to take the mystery out of knowing Christ. Simply put, our game plan has to be intentionally *incarnational* and *invitational*...not only demonstrating God's love in practical ways, but also intentionally inviting people to make the decision to become disciples of Jesus.

Shifts We Must Make as Missional Leaders

From...	To...
"Losing" people from our church	Sending people on God's mission
Giving up our resources	Investing God's provisions
We're too weak	We have authority through Jesus
We can't afford this	We can't afford not to!
One bigger church	More churches reaching more people
Church is for Christians	Ministry for pre-Christians
Ministry for me	I'm a minister for others
Splitting/dividing	Multiplying/expanding
Programs/preferences	Mission-focused ministries meeting needs
My church first	Jesus' mission our first passion
Escape or entertain culture	Engage culture
"Come in here"	"Go out there"
"Come...listen"	"Sent...serving"
Head first	Heart first
Program/institutional	Personal/relational
Start churches/do ministry	Do ministry/start churches

Proclamational	Incarnational and invitational
Believer-focused	Harvest-focused
Church-centered	Community based
Wesley's theology	Wesley's theology *and* methods
"Believe…then you can belong"	"Belong…you'll want to believe"

COACH YOURSELF FORWARD

1. When you look at the words "Christology, Missiology, Ecclesiology," what order would best describe your current personal priorities?
2. What order would best describe your local church's current priorities?
3. What issues need to be addressed in order to have your life and ministry aligned with God's missional priorities?
4. What insights did you gain from the different biblical passages we highlighted? (See Appendix B)
5. How can you begin to apply those insights to your present ministry?
6. What shifts do you need to make in order to be more intentionally missional?
7. What are your next steps to make those shifts?

When Tom and Bill got together again a few weeks later, Bill noticed that Tom was more somber than usual.

"I've been out raising support and haven't been around for about a month," Bill said. "What's been happening since we were together last?"

Tom stirred his coffee for a moment before replying. "I wish I could tell you that everything's been good, but I've run into some unexpected and difficult things lately."

Bill leaned forward, listening intently. "What's been happening?"

Tom shook his head slightly as he looked up at Bill. "You know how excited I've been about the Lord giving me fresh passion for reaching lost people. I want it to become our defining priority as a church so everything we do will align to His Great Commission. I've begun sharing with others what the Lord's been doing in my own heart. I've been sharing with some of our key leaders at church and inviting them to pray with me about how our church could become more intentional about reaching our community. I want to be wise about how I lead our church in light of the shifts we'll need to make in our priorities and ministries."

Bill nodded. "That sounds good, Tom. How have people been responding?"

"That's what's been surprising and somewhat discouraging to me. I thought everyone would be excited with me about joining Jesus on His redemptive mission. Some have been. They have told me that this is just what they've been praying about for us as a church. That's been really encouraging to me. The Holy Spirit has been talking to others about the same things He's been impressing on my heart!" Then Tom shook his head again. "Others...well, the response I've gotten from others wasn't what I expected. Some of my leaders have been doubtful and some actually resistant to reaching lost people. They've been coming up with reasons that just don't make sense."

"I understand," said Bill. "When my wife and I became missionaries, a wise older missionary told us we'd be surprised about who supported us and who didn't. They were right. Some people struggle with change in general. It takes wise leadership to help them move through change in order to follow the Lord into His harvest fields. For others, however, it reveals their true priorities. It's like the principle that Jesus taught in His parable about the tenants in Mark 12—harvest time reveals the heart."

Tom nodded. "I know people process change in different ways. Leading my people through this kind of change will really stretch me as a leader. It won't be easy, but I'm willing to do whatever it takes. However, there have been some other things happening—more than just people's resistance to going beyond what is familiar and comfortable. Things have been happening that are not normal. Some of my leaders tell me that they've been dealing with unusual stresses in their marriage. I've been experiencing more temptation pressure than I have in a long time. One of my kids has suddenly gotten sick and we don't know why. Also, it seems like there's more tension and conflict among people at church lately. It seems like we're under attack or something."

"Harvest time reveals the heart."

"You are under attack," Bill responded. "We went through many similar things on our ministry team. When you become intentional about reaching lost people, you become a special target for Satan. We had a lot to learn about spiritual warfare and the power of prayer. That's why I said that understanding spiritual authority was so important. If the enemy can deter us from pursuing Christ's mission, he's won. When the spiritual resistance is strongest, you're closest to seeing God really break through."

Tom smiled ruefully. "We must be close to a breakthrough then, because the resistance has been really fierce. I really do have a lot to learn about how to deal with that kind of spiritual attack. The devil doesn't fight fair. When he goes after my family and my people like that, I've got to do something about it."

"You don't have to do it alone, Tom. The Lord's got a lot of people He's summoning to be on your team to pray you through this. I'm glad to be on your team!" Bill looked at Tom earnestly. "How are you keeping your intercessors informed and active about these issues?"

For a long moment, Tom was silent, with a look of troubled realization on his face. "Oh...I've forgotten about that! I haven't even developed a prayer team to pray for my family, my ministry and me! I've left us unprotected. That's got to change."

"How are you keeping your intercessors informed and active?"

Bill nodded in agreement. "That's a great insight, Tom. I had to come to the same realization. Prayer that releases the power of God wins the battle. We win first in the unseen realm before we see victory in the visible realm. It sounds like you need to develop a prayer team and a prayer strategy for you and your church."

"That's exactly what I need," Tom replied. "Could we focus our coaching on those issues today?"

"Sounds good," Bill said. "Let's come up with a game plan for prayer."

Together, Tom and Bill identified some options for a prayer team and intercession strategies. Occasionally Bill would share an insight or a story from his own experience, but each time he quickly brought things back to Tom's situation, asking questions that allowed Tom to apply those insights personally.

When they were finished, Tom had several action steps for recruiting his own prayer partners and keeping them informed and active. He also adapted some prayer strategies Bill had used on his mission field and asked Bill to help him train people at church about how to begin praying intentionally for their families, neighbors, work places and community. This time they both captured their ideas in notebooks they had started using during their coaching appointments.

Bill smiled as he watched Tom finish writing down his game plan. As he identified each goal, Bill asked him further questions to refine his action steps.

"Thanks, Bill. I really appreciate how you help me turn my ideas into something that I can actually do. And by the way you are coaching me, I understand better what it means to help someone leave with a game plan that they have created and own themselves."

"Good work, Tom," Bill said. "What we just did was turn your objectives into S-M-A-R-T action steps." He wrote the acronym on a piece of paper. "Here's what we did. We made each action step...

> **S**pecific
> **M**easureable
> **A**ttainable
> **R**elevant
> **T**ime bound

"The difference between having some good ideas and really developing clear action steps is developing your own S-M-A-R-T game plan to move forward."

Tom smiled back. "Thanks for letting me know what you are doing and why you are doing it as you coach me. Do you mind if I use what I'm learning from you with my leaders?"

Bill nodded his agreement. "I was hoping you'd say that. One of the greatest joys I have as a coach is to see leaders like you begin to coach others, too. If it's all right with you, I'd like to not only coach you, but also start equipping you to coach others."

"If I can help my leaders like you're helping me, then it's more than all right. We need this...keep it up!"

Activate Strategic Intercession

Prayer is not just a program. It is the lifestyle of missional leaders and missional churches. Although it's often said that everything rises and falls on leadership, it is more important to recognize that leaders rise or fall on prayer. Intentional missional ministry relies on strategic intercession as its indispensible power source. If you want to love like you've never loved before, lead like you've never led before, care like you've never cared before, share like you've never shared before, go where you've never gone before...then pray like you've never prayed before!

Developing Your Sphere of Intercessors

Developing a prayer team that protects spiritual leaders is often dramatically undervalued. A good model to follow is Jesus' 3-12-70-120 expanding spheres of people. What could your teams of intercessors look like?

- *Your "Inner Circle"*—those who know you best, have the gift of intercession, and are called to pray for you. You can tell them everything—your deepest needs and issues. The inner circle is typically three to five people. Communicate with them often and consider them always "on call" for prayer, no matter what time of day or night. Who are those in your "inner circle"?

- *Your "Twelve"*—people who know you well and you trust to pray often for you. You can share with them almost everything—they will pray for you more than they pray for your project. These people need to be informed regularly. Who are your "twelve"?

- *Your "Extended Community"*—these are people who know you and will occasionally pray for you. They will be interested in general information and requests about your ministry. You will probably communicate with them every one to three months.

An essential priority for leaders is to keep intercessors informed, active and involved. What do you share with your prayer warriors? Here are three areas that inform intercessors:

1. *"News"*—what's happening in your family and ministry. Tell stories of the people you are reaching.
2. *"Numbers"*—share specifics about your results.
3. *"Needs"*—share your personal and ministry needs. If they don't know your needs, they can't pray for specific answers!

Praying for Others

Statistics do tell a story, but for us to truly be gripped by the urgency of the needs of our mission field, numbers must become names.

When a statistic becomes a face we can see and a name that we know… when we see people as lost and truly in danger in the here and now and in the hereafter… when the love of Jesus compels us to go, regardless of the cost… when our mission is that simple and clear—*then* we will define and measure everything we do as a church by whether or not it joins Jesus on His mission in our world and we will pray accordingly.

"My Most Wanted"

1.
2.
3.
4.
5.
6.
7.
8.
9.
10.

If you want to increase the harvest, you've got to intensify your intercession! A useful way to do this is to develop a "My Most Wanted" prayer list. These are the people Jesus has given you a burden to pray for, listen to, serve willingly and share with graciously, so that they might come to know Him, too.

How To B*L*E*S*S Others in Prayer

When we pray for God's Kingdom to come, we are asking the Lord to work in people's lives in such a way that they recognize His powerful love drawing them to know Him. As you take time to get to know people and listen for their needs, the Lord will give you wisdom and authority to pray for them. A prayer strategy I've learned gives a simple guideline to pray specifically and consistently for these key needs in people's lives. Ask the Lord to "bless" people in the following ways:

> *Body*—their physical needs (health issues, addictions, etc.)
> *Labors*—their work (workplace relationships, job needs)
> *Emotions*—their "felt" needs for love, peace, and faith, hope
> *Social*—their relationships with family, friends, neighbors and coworkers
> *Spiritual*—God's best for their lives—His forgiveness, peace, power, and a home in heaven

You can "prayer walk (or drive)" your neighborhood, school, place of work. Pray with His discernment and authority. Ask the Lord of the Harvest for the number of people He wants you to influence for His Kingdom...and ask Him for the faith to do it! God is with you as you pray! Seek to develop a lifestyle of prayer. You will be amazed at the answers to prayer God will bring. Miracles are waiting!

COACH YOURSELF FORWARD

1. How are you developing your intercessory team?
2. How will you help other leaders in your ministry develop their prayer teams?
3. Who's on your "Most Wanted" personal intercession list? Who else might the Lord want you to add?
4. How will you help others identify and begin to intercede intentionally for the people God burdens them to pray for?

5. In what ways can you increase the prayer temperature and involvement in your ministry?
6. In what ways can you be intentional about equipping your people to become intercessors in their neighborhoods, schools and work places?
7. What S-M-A-R-T goals can you develop as a game plan for your ministry of intercession?

FURTHER RESOURCES

Seek God for the City (A Forty Day Guide for the Million Mile Prayer Walk), *www.wesleyan.org/mmpw*

Partners in Prayer by John Maxwell (Thomas Nelson, 1996)

"Coaching Guideline" by Tim Roehl (see Appendix A)

Missional Renaissance by Reggie McNeal (Jossey-Bass, 2009)

TransforMissional Coaching by Tim Roehl and Steve Ogne (Broadman & Hulman Publishing, 2008)

The Celtic Way of Evangelism by George Hunter (Abingdon Press, 2000)

And: The Church Gathered and Scattered by Hugh Halter and Matt Smay (Zondervan, 2010)

Six Word Lessons to Discover Missional Living by Dave DeVries (Leading on the Edge International, 2010)

3

"Studying"

Your Mission Field Redemptively

When Tom and Bill got together again, they spent time celebrating the accomplishments they'd been working on. Tom shared how the Lord was growing his passion for lost people. "Every day the way I view my world is different now," Tom said. "I see people through the Father's eyes and feel His love for them. I long for them to know His forgiveness and freedom. I've been more sensitive and intentional about reaching out to my neighbors. It's been coming through in my conversations and my preaching. I have more confidence as I grow in my identity in Christ and understand spiritual authority. As I share what the Lord's doing in me, it's been exciting to see how He's been doing the same thing for others—people in my church, other pastors in our community and my ministry buddies around the country. Our leaders are catching the vision to make the Great Commission our priority. I can tell the difference now that I have a prayer team interceding for us. As we've begun to pray at church and around our community, opportunities are opening up to us like never before. So many good things have been happening, but I just know there's so much more to come!"

Bill smiled in agreement. "It's good for us to stop, pay attention and celebrate what the Lord's been doing. The journey is long. When we look at how much there is to do, it can be overwhelming. But when we stop and celebrate how far the Lord has brought us, it keeps us encouraged and fuels us to keep on moving ahead. How about if we spend some time just thanking Jesus for what we're celebrating here?"

Tom's response was to bow his head and pour out his heart in thanks and plead with the Lord to trust him and their church for more souls. Bill murmured his agreement and continued with a prayer that blended adoration and authority in a powerful way. The two men basked in the Presence and sensed the reality of what the Psalmist called being "anointed with fresh oil." (Psalm 92:10)

When Tom looked up again, his face was glowing. "Wow...there's nothing like meeting with Jesus like this! Thanks again for walking with me, Bill. And thanks for the message you preached at our church Sunday. I sure appreciated how you helped us understand that we are all missionaries where God has placed us. The way you described the church as disciples making disciples making disciples was powerful. A lot of people talked to me about the way those concepts are reshaping their walk with Jesus and their daily lives. If we are to become missionaries to our own community, I wanted my people to hear your heart, as well as some of the strategies the Lord helped you develop. I'm realizing we have to be spiritual *and* strategic in our ministry. You're helping me pay attention to both."

Bill smiled his thanks. "I appreciate that, Tom. It's not uncommon for leaders to go to an extreme on either side. Some are so spiritual that they think they should just pray and the rest is up to God. That's usually a recipe for inactivity. Others go to the other extreme and make it all about strategy and planning. It becomes all about numbers and our self-effort. I like the old saying that we're supposed to pray as if everything depends on God and work as if everything depends on us. I would observe that we have been mostly paying attention to the spiritual side of things so far in our coaching journey. The Lord has to do His work *in* us to prepare us for the work He wants to do *through* us."

"He's sure been doing a lot in me," said Tom. "I'm hungry for the Lord to do more through me. I've been thinking about how to make the missional shifts we talked about and I've been praying more intentionally for my mission field. I really want to know more about the *missiology* part of our missional priorities. How can I become more intentional about discerning the needs of our mission field? In my ministry training I learned how to exegete Scriptures, but I didn't learn much about how to exegete culture. I need to learn more about how to think and act like a missionary, so we can bring Jesus to our community. How do we do that?"

Bill smiled. "I would agree that we are ready to drill down on that issue now. When I became a missionary, I had a burning desire to bring Christ to the people of our mission field. I thought all I needed to do was to start having services, invite them to come, and do church like I was used to. It was all about getting them to listen to me." He chuckled. "I soon learned that I had things backward again. I needed to listen first. I knew I'd been sent, but I didn't know what I needed to know to help them respond to Jesus. The power of God's call got me there and kept me there, but I had still had a lot to learn."

"That's where I am," said Tom. "But you must have done something right when we look at all the fruit your ministry is bearing in a place most people feel is nearly unreachable. What did you do?"

Bill said, "I was desperate to figure out what to do. Thankfully, the Lord made sure that I met another missionary who became a mentor and a coach to me. That sure made a big difference."

Tom said, "I really appreciate what I'm learning about coaching. It's already making a difference in how I lead others. What's the difference between a mentor and a coach?"

"Good question…and an important distinction," replied Bill. "The simplest way I know to describe the difference between them is this: a mentor pours in and a coach pulls out. When I tell you some of my story or share some ideas with you, that's more mentoring. When I ask questions using our G-R-O-W pathway to help you develop your own game plan, that's coaching."

Tom's eyes lit up with an "aha" of understanding. "That's really helpful. So, would you mind pouring in some of what you learned? I'm a sponge."

Bill laughed. "Sure. As my coach worked with me, I came up with four key words that served as a mental pathway for discerning needs and developing a game plan for our mission field." He pulled out a sheet of paper and wrote,

Sent… Student… Servant… Storyteller

"I feel like I understand the *sent* part now," said Tom. "What do the other words mean?"

"Well," Bill responded. "Before I could tell God's story in a way others could understand and relate to, I had to assume a listening, learning posture and become a student of their culture. My coach helped me identify questions that I needed to ask and then learn about. That's the *student* part. As we discerned needs and opportunities, we then asked the Lord how He wanted us to address those needs and opportunities that fit who we were as a team. That became the *servant* part of our ministry pathway. As we demonstrated God's love in practical ways, He gave us relationship and favor with people. We listened to their stories and began to share ours. We earned the right to have spiritual conversations and invite people to our gatherings, because we focused on *being* the church, rather than *having* church. Then, we were able to determine how to tell God's Good News in ways they could understand and respond to. We learned to translate the gospel for them. We designed our church services and ministries based on how to best relate the story of Jesus for them. That's the *storyteller* part."

"Cool," said Tom, his head nodding in agreement. "It fits right in with your *Christology*, *Missiology*, *Ecclesiology* principles. This is the practical application of those missional priorities, right?"

"Right," said Bill. "The priorities are pretty simple and clear, and the pathway is, too. What you learn and do as a student, servant and storyteller will help you develop a unique game plan for ministry to your mission field." Pointing to the words, he asked, "Where are you right now on that pathway?"

Tom thought for a moment. "Like I said, we are getting a grasp on what it means to be sent. That's influencing all we do. It looks like the next focus for me personally and for us as a church needs to be on studying our mission field. We don't know what we need to know yet, in order to be and bring Good News to our community. You said you came up with some questions that helped you study your mission field. What were they?

"Tell you what," said Bill. "How about if we work on your game plan for that right now? I'm sure the questions you think of will be very similar to mine."

Tom pulled out a sheet of paper. "I know where you're going," he smiled. "Let's do the G-R-O-W and drill down. You pour in some and then pull out of me what we need to do."

They worked through the coaching process together and came up with a list of questions to help Tom study his local mission field redemptively. It included questions such as:

1. What needs does Jesus want us to meet to help bring people to Him?

2. What positive qualities of the culture here can become bridges for the Good News? What negative qualities of the culture here are barriers to overcome?

3. What are the spiritual strongholds holding people in this area back from knowing Jesus?

4. What redemptive gifts does the Lord want to release to this area to set people free?

5. Who knows what we need to know? Check the S*o*I*L—in other words, who are the "Sphere of Influence Leaders" in this area who can give us perspective?

6. Who are the people of peace God wants us to meet?

7. Who are the intercessors and other spiritual leaders in this area that we can join with in ministry?

Afterwards, Bill and Tom developed several approaches Tom and his team could use to answer each question.

Tom looked up from the extensive notes he had captured. "I really like this. It makes me wonder why we haven't been doing these things before!" He pointed to one item on his list. "I'm especially excited about this checking the S*o*I*L idea."

Bill said, "It's always gratifying to see how the Holy Spirit goes ahead of us. I'll be interested to know what you learn from your listening and where you find what I like to call 'receptive soil.' You are going to find that the Lord of the Harvest already has a game plan for you. It will unfold itself as the Spirit leads you, and that will become your strategy."

Tom smiled. "I believe that. As we study our mission field redemptively, let's pray that we'll learn what He wants us to know! Lead out, Bill, will you?"

Bill's response was to ask the Lord for His wisdom, favor and discernment for Tom and his team. Both men had a sense of anticipation that some wonderful conversations and discoveries were coming.

Gather Statistical Insights

Demographic research provides a valuable overview of your mission field for discerning the needs and opportunities around you. Websites such as *www.percept.com*, *www.city-data.com,* or *www.easidemographics.com* are good starting places.

Your research will require limiting the scope of your study. Through prayer, determine the size of your "parish" or "circle of accountability." In a densely populated area, your parish may be smaller geographically, but broader ethnically. You may feel led to focus especially on a particular segment of your parish. As you review demographic facts, pay attention to the issues that will help develop a profile of the needs of people in your area. Pastor Rick Warren of Saddleback Church in California used this kind of study to develop a description of a typical resident of his community that he nicknamed "Saddleback Sam." Statistical information creates a clear picture of those you are called to reach.

What do demographic statistics tell you about your mission field in the following areas?

- **Ethnic diversity**—What different ethnic groups live here? Who is the majority group(s)? Who are the minorities? How many languages are spoken? How has the population changed over the past ten years in terms of numbers and ethnicity? What are the projections for the next ten years?
- **Economic issues**—What are the median income and income range in your area? How would your area be described in terms of income and lifestyles?
- **Employment**—What different kinds of employment are in the area? Who are the major employers? What is the mix of "white collar", "blue collar" and "no collar" (information and technology) jobs in your area? What is the unemployment rate? How far do people drive to work?

- **Education**—What are the different schools in the area? What is the average level of education?
- **Entertainment**—What kind of entertainment businesses are there? How many of them are harmful to healthy families and communities? Where and how do people spend their money? What recreation facilities are in the area?
- **Environment**—How will ministry in this area be affected by local geography, politics and social attitudes?
- **Family make-up**—How many are married? Single? What percentage of people fit into the different ages and stages of life (such as children, teens, young adults, senior citizens, etc.)? How many single parent families are there?
- **Churches**—What kinds of churches or spiritual centers of other religions are in the area? What does that tell you?

As you review the demographic information further, what are other insights you should note? Ask the Holy Spirit to point out what He wants you to focus on.

After you review these initial demographic findings, what are your impressions about the kinds of churches and ministries needed by people in your area?

Survey Spiritual Dynamics

When doing spiritual survey work (some call this spiritual mapping), we are seeking to discern the spiritual dynamics and influences of our mission field. What we can't see statistically is manifested in the attitudes and actions of people. Spiritual surveying further informs our intercession and helps form ministry strategies.

As you "map" your mission field, exegete the culture (which some simply define as "the way we do things around here") from two key perspectives:

First, what are the good qualities of this culture that we can use as bridges for the Good News? Second, what are the qualities of this culture corrupted by sin that are barriers we must overcome?

Begin your spiritual survey work by doing prayer walks or prayer drives around your area. Just be out among people! As you walk or drive, record your observations or impressions. Ask the Lord to give you His perspective, so you can "see" with His eyes and heart.

Another key part of doing spiritual survey work is to ask the Lord to lead you to people with spiritual discernment about your area. They are often doing the quiet, somewhat hidden, work of intercession. Some have a long history in your area. Ask other spiritual leaders in the community who the local prayer warriors are that they have already discovered. Some may be in your congregation; some may be in other churches. Many will be women. "Praying grannies" are well known in heaven! When you find them, listen closely to their wisdom and benefit from the power of their prayer lives.

Here are some important means of seeking discernment, while doing your spiritual survey work.

1. **Pray!** Ask God to give you understanding of the strongholds of the enemy, the needs of the people, and the redemptive possibilities He has in mind.

2. Review the **past.** As you study the history of your area, you will begin to discern the spiritual influences at work. What important events have taken place? Who were the pioneers of the area? What were their intentions and priorities for this area? What attitudes and behaviors have long been part of the culture?

3. Look at significant **places.** Pay attention to the houses, yards, decorations, signs, businesses and public spaces. How well do people take care of things? Look for monuments, the layout of the area, statues, spiritual places...anything that might help you identify spiritual influences and idols.

4. Look for the seats of **power**. Get to know the government, business, education and religion centers. Who are the key people in positions of power in the area? What are their attitudes toward the things of God? Some communities are highly resistant to God's work. Others (sometimes neighborhoods in a different part of a city or across a geographic boundary) are open and receptive to the Lord. Seek to discern the reasons for those attitudes.

5. What are the **practices** of the community? What are the main festivals or celebrations? What types of activities do many people participate in? What brings people together? What divides them? Pay attention to sports and recreation leagues, community groups, niche groups, etc. These help us understand the values and priorities of the people in your mission field.

6. Learn about spiritual **problems** you need to address. What kinds of influence are there from other religions, cults or occult groups? What holds people back from finding God? Find out what people believe in your area. Beliefs influence behavior. Although people's theological views are important, the best place to understand problems will be in the descriptions of more tangible issues around people's physical, material and emotional needs. Learn to listen for people's longings. That's when we are really hearing them on their heart level. As you listen to their longings, you'll better understand what others believe about the essential issues of Christian faith, such as God, Jesus Christ, the Bible, heaven, hell, sin, salvation, church… as well as unusual religious practices, such as praying for or to the dead, idols, New Age practices, etc.

7. Listen to, link with and pray with your Kingdom **partners**. What other churches are in the area? Get to know other pastors. Listen to their insights. What is the spiritual condition of other churches? How is the spiritual unity

among pastors? What issues do they feel hinder the work of the Kingdom in their area? Find your teammates, ask for their blessing as you join God's team in your area and pray with them!

As you get to know the area, prayerfully take note of two major issues. First, list the *spiritual strongholds* (such as hopelessness, fear, poverty, self-righteousness, pleasure seeking, tradition, addiction, etc.) that identify the problems you must address in order to meet needs in your community. A spiritual stronghold is an ingrained attitude of hopelessness, based on a lie from Satan that keeps people bound in sin and separated from God. Second, list the *redemptive gifts* God wants to bless the area with—His possibilities! Ask the Lord to show you assets that can be leveraged for redemptive purposes. What ministries can you develop to meet people's needs and break strongholds? A redemptive gift is a supernatural release of power from God that brings His redemption to people that liberates those held captive by strongholds.

*Check the "S*o*I*L" (Sphere of Influence Leaders)*

Statistics are helpful and spiritual survey work is vital, but listening to real people is what makes ministry truly personal. Get to know individuals in your community. Prayerfully walk among the people of your mission field, asking God to show you their needs through His eyes. Talk with the people of your mission field, humbly seeking friendships as one who wants to learn. As you do, the Lord will do amazing things! Listening enables us to discern where the Lord is already at work. Troy Evans, pastor of The Edge in Grand Rapids, Michigan, encourages leaders to "learn from indigenous wisdom" (*The Edge of Redemption*, Wesleyan Publishing House, 2011).

Key missional questions to ask as you study your mission field are:

- What needs does Jesus want us to meet in order to bring more people to Him?

- What local assets and relationships could the Lord use redemptively?
- Who knows what we need to know?
- What's not being done in our area that we could do?
- Who are the "persons of peace"?
- What could be our Kingdom niche and unique contribution to His work in this area?

As you listen, two types of individuals will be especially helpful: "Persons of Peace" and "Sphere of Influence Leaders" (S*o*I*L). A person of peace is someone who has influence in the area, whether they have an official title or not. They can open doors to large networks of relationships, influence and service opportunities. A biblical example of a person of peace is Lydia in Acts 16:11-16. Finding partners like these is essential!

There are other key leaders to whom you will want to listen also. Think of them as "Sphere of Influence Leaders" in your mission field. Here are some examples of the different types of "S*o*I*L" you may find. You can add more to the list.

1. *Education*—school leaders
2. *Law enforcement*—police chief, sheriff, etc.
3. *Government*—mayor, city/county officials, city planners, etc.
4. *Spiritual leaders*—pastors and parachurch leaders...our Kingdom teammates
5. *Business leaders*—Chamber of Commerce, Rotary, etc.
6. *Social service agencies*
7. *Media*—publishers, radio/TV, etc.
8. *Subcultures*—leaders in niche groups like partiers, bikers, ethnic groups, etc.
9. *Realtors and builders*
10. *Community organizations*—groups of people who meet because of a common interest, such as Chamber of Commerce, Rotary, support groups, hobbies or other special interests

11. *Sports and recreation organizations*
12. The *"Bishop"*—the most influential spiritual leader of the area to learn from
13. *"Divine appointments"*—watch for people God sends to you!
14. "Niche" groups that may be unique to your area

What are the names of leaders representing these various spheres of influence? As you find out, pray for them. Ask the Lord to help you find "receptive soil." Call those on your list. Tell them that your church wants to become a better servant to your community and you are interested in learning from them. Ask them if you could have about a half-hour of their time. Often, these kinds of leaders are pleasantly surprised when they meet church leaders who want to listen before they speak. Remember, be gracious and be brief. If they appear interested and want to give you more time, take advantage of their generosity and learn much.

Here's a sample survey for these sphere of influence leaders.

1. How would you describe this area to a new person just moving in? What are our greatest strengths?
2. From your position as a leader of influence in this area, what do you see as our greatest needs?
3. What are some ways a church that wants to be a servant to our area could partner with agencies like yours to help others?
4. What advice would you give me as a new spiritual leader in our community?
5. Who else would you recommend that I talk to that could help me learn more?
6. How can I pray for you or your family? How can we serve you?
7. Thanks for your time! May we update you on our progress?

After you've done your "Check the S*O*I*L" interviews, bring your team together to share and pray about what you've learned. Glean the key issues from those conversations as indicators of how the Lord is leading you to engage your community redemptively.

COACH YOURSELF FORWARD

1. What did you learn from the demographic statistics about your mission field? Draw a "map" of your mission field, capturing the main boundaries and key insights from those statistics.
2. As you look at the "spiritual map" of your area, what are the spiritual dynamics you need to address in prayer? How will you keep your intercessors informed and active?
3. What are the strongholds/needs of your mission field? What are some ways you can address them?
4. What are the redemptive gifts/ministry opportunities you are discovering? What are some ways you can activate them?
5. Draw a picture that describes the heart profile of the needs, values, and dreams of the people of your mission field.
6. In light of what you have discovered and discerned, what types of ministries might you develop?
7. What kinds of teams will you need for those ministries?

FURTHER RESOURCES

Percept, *www.perceptgroup.com*

EASI Demographics, *www.easidemographics.com*

www.City-Data.com

Breaking the Missional Code by Ed Stetzer (Broadman & Hulman Publishers, 2006)

"Spy Teams" (see Appendix C)

4

"Shaping"

Your Church for Missional Engagement

"Wow...we didn't know how much we needed to know!" exclaimed Tom, as he and Bill met for their next coaching visit.

"I can't wait to hear what your team's been learning and process those discoveries with you," said Bill. "Before we focus on our mission field here, I'm curious what you've been hearing from your ministry buddies. You told me that you have been sharing what we've been doing with them. How have they been adapting these principles and practices in their ministry settings?"

Tom leaned forward smiling. "They've been really excited. You know how diverse their ministry environments are. Yet, it doesn't seem to matter whether they are urban, suburban, rural, small church, large church or a new church. They all tell me that because this isn't a one size fits all program, they are developing and personalizing a game plan for their unique mission field." Tom grinned. "I've been also been telling them about G-R-O-W as a coaching path you've been using with me. They've started using it with their leaders. And we're starting to coach each other. It's fun! Coaching isn't as easy as you make it look, though. I need to learn more about how to do it."

"You're already making good progress in your coaching skills. I'm glad your buddies are finding what we're doing here helpful for what they are doing there," said Bill. "Thanks for the update. So, what would you like to focus on today?"

"Well, like I said, we didn't know how much we needed to know until we decided to become students of our mission field," replied Tom. "There's so much we learned! There are so many needs! I want to figure out what the Lord wants us to do with what we've learned. What needs are we supposed to address? What ministries should we develop? What does Jesus want us to do?"

"Great questions. Could I add another that might help us with our goal for today?" With Tom's affirmative nod, he continued, "What needs are you and your church best suited to meet?"

Tom sat thoughtfully. "That's a great question. I'm not sure. What's the best way to figure that out?"

"The Holy Spirit is very wise in the way He leads," said Bill. "We'll have to discern what needs He wants us to focus on in the community. At the same time, what He wants us to do outside the church will also fit who He's brought together in our church. So, let's see how He's shaped our church to meet the needs of our mission field."

"It will be a blend of what we've learned about our mission field and what we learn about ourselves," Tom said.

"Right. Let's get a picture of the needs that consistently rose to the surface in your study and that you sense the Lord leading you to address. We can't minister to every need out there, but there are definitely some the Lord can use us to meet."

Tom pulled out a paper and spread it out so they could both see it. "Here's a synthesis of what we've learned so far. The S*o*I*L interviews were especially helpful." He pointed to a short list on the page. "These needs are things we heard consistently. We've especially been praying about them."

"Great work," commented Bill. He pulled out a fresh piece of paper. "Let's see how those needs fit who we are as a church." He wrote "Mission Field Needs" on one side of the page and "Our Ministry Strengths" on the other side, forming two columns. "Let's write the needs the Lord is highlighting for us and then see how He might use our gifts and skills as strengths to meet them."

"We've done some study of spiritual gifts in our church," commented Tom. "But I'm afraid to say we looked at gifts more from the perspective of ministry in the Body than from engaging our mission field."

"Knowing how the power of God works in and through us is vital," said Bill. "Our ministry profile helps shape our ministries. We will bear fruit best where we fit and flourish in ministry." Bill smiled at Tom. "Where do you best fit and flourish?"

"Fit and flourish. What do you mean by that?" asked Tom.

"Well, there are different ways to say it," said Bill. "Some call it their 'sweet spot'. Another way would be to describe it as when you most often experience God's power, joy and fruit in your life. Others call it your ministry profile. Where you fit and flourish is a blend of a number of factors."

"I understand. What would those factors be?" asked Tom.

Bill's eyes twinkled and he smiled. "What factors do you think are important?"

Tom grinned. "Okay, coach. Let's talk about that and see what we can come up with."

Together, Bill and Tom compiled a list of ways Tom could describe and clarify his sweet spot. It included thinking about his "natural wiring" (personality and leadership style), supernatural empowerment (spiritual gifts), competencies (talents and skills), life experiences and successes, and his ministry burdens and passions. They even talked about Tom's interests and hobbies that could be leveraged more redemptively.

Tom's face showed his excitement. "This is great! I wish I had understood the idea fit and flourish earlier. It would have made a big difference in how I used my time and energy."

Bill said, "My good missionary friend, Paul Ford, says that at least two-thirds of our time in ministry should be spent where we fit and flourish. If we don't, it will drain us and we'll burn out quicker. We won't be as fruitful. And, we may hinder someone else from serving in their sweet spot."

A look of realization came across Tom's face. "I'm spending too much time where I'm not effective. I need to adjust my ministry so I can give the majority of my energy to my strengths. Beyond that, I need to help others find their sweet spots. Imagine how powerful our church would be if our people were all equipped and released in ministries where they fit and flourished!"

"Now you've got it. How could you do that?"

Tom smiled. "Let's coach ourselves to a game plan for that."

"Way to go!" Bill said as they reviewed Tom's action steps. "May I add one more dimension to what we just did?" At Tom's nod, Bill said, "We've just helped you and your people know how to discover your sweet spots personally. How can we do the same thing for the church corporately so that we match our strengths with our mission field's needs?"

"Good thought," said Tom. "We've covered a lot of ground today. Do you mind taking some more time? I'd like to bring all these things together so I can take them back to our leadership team at church and work this through with them."

"Let's go for it," agreed Bill. By the time they finished, Tom had a game plan that addressed several vital areas:

1. Tom would adjust his schedule so he could invest more time where he fit and flourished.
2. Tom would work with his leaders to help them discover their sweet spots.
3. Their church would do a ministry profile to help leverage its strengths and address some areas of concern.
4. They would discern how to match the needs of their mission field with their strengths as a church, staying sensitive to the leading of the Spirit as they developed teams.
5. Tom would share his notes with his ministry friends so they could adapt them for their use.

"Whew...we made great progress, but there's a lot of work ahead. The pieces are coming together, though. It makes me more dependent on the Lord than ever!" exclaimed Tom.

Bill nodded. "That's a wonderful place to live... desperately dependent on Jesus! It reminds me of a verse that has encouraged me many times from Philippians 2:13. 'For it is God who works in you to will and to act in order to fulfill His good purpose.'"

"Let's claim that as we pray," said Tom. They did.

Let Your Mission Field Shape Your Vision

We've been learning that a church's vision often starts in the hearts of its leaders, but is shaped by its mission field as well. Here are some ways the mission field impacts vision and ministry strategies.

First, if the number of people in your mission field who are unchurched is about 80% (based on research by David Olson in *The American Church in Crisis*), how many people does that represent in the geographic area the Lord has made you responsible for? By faith, what percent of those people will you claim for Christ? For example, if there are 10,000 people in your mission field, about 8,000 of them are currently unchurched. If you claimed one percent of them for Christ, your goal would be to see 80 people become disciples of Jesus. If you become a five percent church, you'd be claiming 400 people to come to Christ. What is the Lord calling you to claim?

Second, estimate how many people your church has the potential to touch tangibly with the love of Jesus in some way? What number is the Lord inviting you to claim through your ministries and the influence of your people where they live and work?

Third, when you compare the redemptive opportunities of your mission field with your church's sweet spots and strengths, how does that further shape your vision?

COACH YOURSELF FORWARD

1. How many people in your mission field are unchurched? (Hint: The national average is about 80% of the population in your area, but you should be able to be more specific, based on your own local religious demographics research.)
2. How many of that number is the Lord inviting you to claim? How many will become new disciples of Jesus because of your ministry? One percent? Five percent? Ten percent?
3. How many people are within the "sphere of influence" of the people of your church? How many people could your church touch at least once a year with the love of Jesus in some practical way?
4. How can you incorporate these ministry goals into your intercession strategy?

Learn How You Fit and Flourish

There is great power in leading people to discovery and clarity about how they best fit and flourish! Develop a game plan to help you and your people realize their sweet spot or ministry profile. Here are some factors to consider:

1. *Natural wiring*—personality or leadership style
2. *Supernatural empowerment*—spiritual gifts
3. *Competencies*—talents and skills
4. *Fruit*—effectiveness, past successes and fruitfulness
5. *Passion*—ministry burden or vision
6. *History*—life experiences the Lord can use redemptively
7. *Interests*—hobbies or relational connections

Not only is it important to help each person develop their ministry profile, it's also important to see how our individual sweet spots come together to form God's team. Veteran missionary Paul Ford of Church Resource Ministries (CRM) reminds us that we must pay attention to both "me" and "we" in order to understand how the Body of Christ can be healthy and effective in missional ministry. There are a number of great resources that can help you and others do self-assessment.

Personality Tools—Google to check out survey instruments, like the DiSC Profile, the Taylor-Johnson Temperament Analysis, Myers-Briggs, or StrengthsFinder. You'll find these and other tools useful for providing insights for identifying individual personality characteristics. Each has a practical, yet distinct, approach for helping people understand how they relate to others, process information, manage conflict, handle stress and view life overall.

Spiritual Gifts—There are inventories and assessment surveys specifically designed to help users identify and explore their spiritual gifts—in other words, how the power of the Holy Spirit lifts us beyond our natural personality and skills to operate in supernatural ways. Paul Ford's *Your Leadership Grip* helps people see their spiritual gifts from three angles—their personal gift mix, how their gifts function in a team setting, and how their gifts function in the Body of Christ for redemptive purposes. The *APEST* assessment, developed by Alan Hirsh, is a subjective profiling instrument, designed to assist you in finding your ministry style in relation to the philosophy of the fivefold ministry mentioned in Ephesians chapter four, involving Apostles (who ensure that the faith is transmitted from one context to another and from one generation to the next), Prophets (who bring correction, challenge dominant cultural assumptions, and help the community to obey what God has commanded), Evangelists (who are infectious communicators of the gospel that recruit others to follow Christ and to engage in His mission of growing the church), Shepherds (who nurture, protect and develop disciples in the community of faith), and Teachers (who understand and explain God's truth and wisdom so that the Church remains on a foundation of sound doctrine).

Tools That Blend Several Areas—Here are some tools that are designed to help people see their natural, supernatural and practical characteristics as they relate to ministry in the body of Christ.

Discovering Your Ministry Identity by Paul Ford

Grip Birkman Blueprint tool

Network developed by Willow Creek

SHAPE developed by Saddleback

Assess Your Team Collectively

In addition to individual assessment, it's also important to evaluate leadership teams and congregations to know whether they are healthy and where they may need to address concerns. The *Church Health Profile* (CHP) is designed especially for churches that function in a denominational setting. It examines twelve church health factors and is an online assessment tool available at *www.churchhealthprofile.com*. Other church health survey tools are also useful, such as the Natural Church Development (NCD) survey, which helps churches identify "minimum factors" to address from among eight areas of church vitality.

Regardless of the profile instrument used, some essential elements have to be in place for a missional church health process to be effective. First, be clear about the purpose for the process. Clarity about mission produces passion and urgency. The Church's primary purpose is to "fulfill the Great Commandment in the Spirit of the Great Commission." Our singular aspiration is summed up in the words of Jesus: "The Son of Man has come to seek and save the lost...and give them life to the fullest" (Luke 19:10; John 10:10).

Our focus must be on making disciples who make disciples. A missional health process requires wise, courageous leadership! Church leaders must commit to a process that will take place over a period of months, not just settle for getting scores from a survey or doing an event. Willingness to be accountable through the process from the very beginning is essential.

Second, do a comprehensive profile. The goal is to get a clear picture of the local church that includes input from external and objective sources, as well as the personal insights of church members. Do an objective evaluation with a tool such as the Wesleyan Church Health Profile or Natural Church Development survey. These instruments help "paint the picture" of a church's overall health. An onsite consultation, led by a professional consultant or team, will look at issues such as history, facilities, attendance and financial statistics, the church's mission field and policies, as well as insights from church members. Written results should be shared with the pastor, leaders and people, providing a clearer picture of reality—including strengths to celebrate; issues to address; recommendations with clear outcomes that will translate into goals; and responses in the form of commitments of the pastor, leaders and people to see the process through to completion.

Third, develop practical steps for implementation. As you process the information, further personalize the recommendations by developing clear outcomes and goals all tied to your mission and mission field. Your game plan should celebrate and leverage strengths and also address key areas of concern or "minimum factors." Develop both a church health plan and a missional game plan to engage your mission field. "Health" and "harvest" go together! Empower prayer and health teams. Keep your intercessors informed and active! Empower your health team to work with your leadership team. Clearly communicate who has the ability to make recommendations and decisions. The process needs to be pastor-led and supported and protected by district or judicatory leaders. Coaching is essential. Incorporate training throughout the process to equip leaders to reach missional goals. Determine to get into a regular rhythm of life as a church and go through this kind of missional health process every year or two.

"Health" and "harvest" go together!

A missional game plan will focus your church on bringing Jesus to your community. Assessing leaders and churches so they know where they best fit and flourish in this process is a vital part of developing an intentional missional plan!

COACH YOURSELF FORWARD

1. Assessment is a key part of a wholistic, healthy church multiplication A*C*T*N plan (Assessment, Coaching, Training, Networking). How will you help individuals in your church know how they can best fit and flourish?
2. How will you assess your church's collective health? How will you make sure it is integrated into a missional game plan?

Link Community Needs with Church Strengths

Connecting the gifts and skills the Lord has given your team with the needs of your mission field takes a blend of both spiritual and strategic wisdom. Prayerfully list the needs and opportunities of your mission field, alongside the strengths and sweet spots of your church. Paul Ford says, "Let's see who God has brought to see what God intends to do through us." Here are some questions to help you process these issues.

- What have we learned from "Checking the S*o*I*L"?
- What needs does Jesus want us to meet?
- What assets and opportunities are in the community that we could leverage for redemptive purposes?
- What ministry teams do we have in our church that could address these needs?
- What mission teams could we develop to bring Good News to our community?
- What kinds of leaders will we need for these teams?

Develop a side-by-side list of the "Needs and Opportunities of Our Mission Field" with the "Strengths and Sweet Spots of Our Church."

There are many things your church *could* do. Ask the Lord what *He* wants you to do as your top priorities! Veteran coach and CRM missionary Steve Ogne offers three good questions for discerning missional activities to invest in:

1. How well does this activity make a difference by meeting real needs?
2. How well does this activity help us build relationships?
3. How well does this activity help us make disciples?

Empower Ministry and Mission Teams

Now consider the teams needed for the ministries your church will develop. There are two kinds of teams to consider: current *Ministry Teams* already in your church that could become more missional, and *Mission Teams* that will allow even more people to get involved in ministry outside your church.

When it comes to your church's current ministries, look at them from three perspectives:

1. Which ministries help your people go deep with God?
2. Which help your people go deep with others?
3. Which ministries help your people go deep into the harvest?

Think about how to make your existing ministries more intentionally missional. For example, the worship team could begin doing music sets at a local coffee place. Your hospitality team could serve lunch to area business leaders or teachers at a local school. Your nursery and children's ministry teams could do a "Parent's Night Out" that allows moms and dads some time for a date or shopping while the church ministers to their kids. There are many creative ways that ministry teams can become more effective, relational bridges to your community, while building up those who are already in Christ.

External mission teams focus on serving the needs and opportunities of our mission field. As they do, they provide new possibilities for people to get involved. There are untapped and underutilized people resources in your church and community! Prayerfully develop a list of new teams you can deploy in your missional game plan. For a worksheet that deals with developing Ministry and Mission Teams, see Appendix D.

Look for Team Leaders

There is a lot of good information available today about leadership and teams. Raising up and equipping leaders for your ministry and mission teams is an essential part of multiplying ministry effectiveness. Who you choose to invest your time in is a crucial issue. Here's a simple way to categorize the different kinds of people in your church:

"Moochers" drain time and energy. They often have special needs that require healing before they can contribute to the

mission. Develop ministries for them where they can learn to help each other, such as support groups.

"Members" are nice people who attend and often appreciate what you do, but don't contribute much to the mission. They may be waiting to be invited to find how they can fit and flourish.

"Ministers" are willing to serve and have abilities in particular areas. They make great team members or can do specific ministries well on their own.

"Multipliers" have the capacity to recruit others to a vision, equip them, build teams and multiply themselves. They are a great resource to your ministry!

"Missionaries" can contribute for a short season in specific ways. They may come to your church to help, but not feel led to stay long-term. These leaders are especially important in starting new churches. Your church may also send out missionaries to help ministries outside your church locally or even globally!

As you look at the human resources in your church and the teams you need, look especially for multipliers! These people are like diamonds...fairly rare and very valuable. Learn to look for potential multipliers...sometimes they are diamonds in the rough, just waiting to be encouraged and equipped among the people of your church (young and old). Ask the Lord to help you see them!

COACH YOURSELF FORWARD

1. List the ministries of your church according to the three areas we identified:
   a. Ministries that help your people go deep with God.
   b. Ministries that help your people go deep with each other.

     c.   Ministries that help your people go deep into the harvest.

2. As you review your ministries from these perspectives, what do you notice? How balanced are your ministries? What might you need to adjust? How can you view all your ministries through a missional lens in order to align them with God's missional purposes?

3. Comparing your mission field's needs with the strengths of your church, what connections and possibilities do you see? Which are the Holy Spirit prioritizing for you?

4. As we look at your existing ministry teams and potential mission teams, how can they be better aligned with your missional game plan? How could these teams partner with existing groups or organizations outside your church?

5. In what ways can your current ministry teams become more missional? What might you need to stop doing so you can start doing ministry according to the Holy Spirit's priorities?

6. How will you bring together the new teams you need for missional ministries? Who are your ministers and multipliers? How will you equip and release them?

7. As you look at the people of your church, who is the Holy Spirit pointing out for you to invest in? Who is outside your church that could be invited to be on one of your teams?

8. Who are the younger leaders God is raising up? How might you include them?

FURTHER RESOURCES

Personality Tools

DiSC Profile, www.discprofile.com

Taylor Johnson Temperament Analysis, www.tjta.com

Myers-Briggs Type Indicator, www.mbticomplete.com

StrengthsFinder, www.strengthsfinder.com

Spiritual Gifts

Your Leadership Grip by Paul Ford (ChurchSmart Resources, 2007)

APEST Profile by Allan Hirsh, *www.theforgottenways.org/apest*

Tools That Blend Several Areas

Discovering Your Ministry Identity: For Teams, Groups or Individuals, Learning to Be Who You Already Are by Paul Ford (ChurchSmart Resources, 1998)

Grip Birkman Blueprint Tool at *www.gripbirkmanblueprint.com*

Network by Bruce Bugbee, Don Cousins and Wendy Seidman (Zondervan, 2005)

S.H.A.P.E.: Finding and Fulfilling Your Unique Purpose for Life by Erik E. Rees (Zondervan, 2006)

Five Things Anyone Can Do to Lead Effectively by Phil Stevenson (Wesleyan Publishing House, 2007)

Doing Church as a Team by Wayne Corderio (Regal Books, 2004)

5

"Serving"

that Meets Needs and Opens Doors

As he did with each coaching visit, Bill took time to listen, care and celebrate what was going on in Tom's life. He checked in with him about his walk with Jesus, how his family was doing, how things were going at church and progress made on his action steps from their last visit.

"I appreciate how you take time to see how I'm doing when we meet," Tom commented. "I know we are working on ministry issues, but I can tell that you care about me personally, not just about bottom line performance."

"Glad you noticed," said Bill. "Coaching is a holistic relationship that cares about the person, not just the projects they are working on. Remember, our goal as coaches is to come alongside leaders so they are transformed into the image

The Coach's Four C's:

Clarifying calling

Cultivating character

Creating community

Connecting to culture

of Jesus and join Him on His redemptive mission. That brings the Great Commandment and the Great Commission together in all we do. When we get together, I'm paying attention to what I call the "Four C's"—clarifying calling, cultivating character, creating community and connecting to culture."

"What we've been doing recently has sure made a big difference in clarifying my calling," replied Tom. "What a difference it makes living in my sweet spot! I've been thrilled to see the response of our people as we help them discover where they best fit and flourish. As they realize how Jesus designed them to make a unique contribution to His kingdom purposes, the level of excitement and engagement in our church is increasing in wonderful ways."

"It all fits together, doesn't it?" said Bill. "As we see the mission field through the Father's eyes, we are connected to a great, compelling vision and mission. When we clarify our call so we understand that we all have a place on God's team, we appreciate each other more and create a healthy community. When we join Jesus on His mission and see people's lives transformed, it fuels us and keeps us fresh. A church full of people that know who they are, why they're here, and where they're going is contagious!"

"That's what we're finding out," returned Tom. "There have been lots of bumps along the way, but knowing that Jesus is using us to change people's lives, both now and forever, makes it worth it. It also keeps us praying and dependent on Him!"

"We can't do anything without the purifying, maturing and empowering work of the Holy Spirit, that's for sure," Bill said. "What do you want to focus on today?"

"We've made great progress in understanding the needs of our mission field and the ways our church can develop ministries to meet those needs," said Tom. "We're getting clear about the *why* of our mission and the *who* and *what* of our mission field. Now, we're trying to figure out the *how* and *when*. We've also had some people asking about how our current ministries fit into all this, especially our Sunday morning services. There have been some interesting conversations about how to connect ministry outside our church with what we are already doing inside. We are realizing that the bridges we are building have to create a flow of relationships in two ways—for us to go to our community and for them to come to us. We need to work on being more intentional about those bridges."

"You have been doing a good job of discerning what needs you are best suited to meet and who the Lord is sending you to serve," Bill commented. "How can you be more intentional about when you will serve and who you will serve with? Those issues involve designing a missional calendar and discerning who your missional partners might be. As you work on those issues, perhaps you will discover more ways to develop the missional bridges you mentioned."

Tom nodded thoughtfully. "Calendar, partners, bridges...those sound like key issues to focus on. Let's figure out a game plan to wisely meet needs and opens doors. I'm ready to see how the Lord leads us today!"

Design a Missional Calendar

As leaders discern needs in their community, they must develop ways to demonstrate God's love by meeting those needs in practical, tangible ways that gain credibility for their message. Just like a missionary, we have to "earn the right to be heard" in the culture and venues where we live! Rather than only trying to create events to invite people to come and attend (attractional), we find events and venues where people already are and find ways we can go and serve there (missional). We must be intentional about bridging our service to more opportunities for ministry connections. A key principle is "Where people congregate, we will operate."

Watch for God's divine appointments and open doors. Ask how you can help and find ways to serve in your community. Then, go...love...serve! As you do, God will give you favor and relationships with people. Listen to their story. Learn more about those needs. Keep serving them in love and you'll find spiritual conversations happening naturally...and supernaturally!

But What About Sunday?

It's common for church planters and pastors to ask about how regular church activities, especially Sunday services, fit into a missional game plan. In reality, churches spend most of their energy on their Sunday experience...Sunday school classes, children's church and especially on a worship service. What we do on Sunday is necessary, but not sufficient for a missional game plan. We often put almost all our disciple-making eggs into one Sunday basket! We have to expand the ways we are building bridges, so we can make disciples who make disciples.

A word picture, borrowed from Steve Ogne and Dave DeVries, illustrates this point well. In the game of chess, the most powerful piece on the board is the queen. Many inexperienced players rely heavily on the queen, using it as the primary piece to win the game. However, there are many other pieces on the board that are also important. A good chess player learns to use all the pieces as part of a winning game plan. Sometimes novice chess players are encouraged to learn to play without the queen. When they learn to use the other pieces well, it makes the queen even more powerful as part of a comprehensive game plan. In essence, in order to really play chess well, you first have to learn to play without the queen.

From a church ministry perspective, the "queen" is our Sunday morning worship service. We tend to overuse the queen! When we try to make our Sunday morning worship services accomplish everything—evangelism, worship, discipleship, teaching and fellowship—we are not using the other pieces on our board. It's important to have a great Sunday experience that translates the Good News for new people (more about that later), but it's even more important to build bridges out into the community that make it easier for people to come into church. Remember, an effective game plan is both missional and attractional, but makes being missional the priority.

If you are a planting a church, there will be a lot of pressure to "start having church," which means "start having Sunday morning services." Focusing too much on Sunday can hinder you from equipping your people to be out in the community making disciples through missional ministries. Learn to play without the queen—don't start Sunday services too soon. Utilize the other pieces on your board—making disciples through strategic prayer, incarnating the gospel through service, relationship building, creating small groups or missional communities, checking the "S*o*I*L" and living a missional lifestyle. Then, when you add the "queen"—your Sunday morning ministries—you'll do it as part of a comprehensive missional game plan.

If you are pastoring an existing church, help people see that a missional game plan will add to your effectiveness, not take away from what you are already doing. Your goal is to make sure that what you do on Sunday is integrated into what you are doing the rest of the week out in your community. If you do, all the "pieces on the board"—the players on your teams—will be more effective...and you'll have more people in the game!

As you seek to be strategic and spiritually sensitive in developing your missional game plan, "calendar" ministry that is intentional about developing *attractional*, *incarnational* and *invitational* ministry. A key is to be sensitive to "receptive" and aware of the "resistant" times on the calendar of people's lives. Here are several considerations to keep in mind.

"Church" Calendar

The spiritual holidays of Christmas and Easter are still two times of the year when many unchurched people are open to coming to "church." More liturgical congregations are very conscious of the

Christian calendar, while other churches virtually ignore it. Whether unchurched or dechurched, the realities of Christ's incarnation, crucifixion and resurrection highlight the distinct uniqueness of Jesus as Lord. Planning ministries inside and outside your church during these receptive seasons of the "church" calendar can reap great harvest results.

"Culture" Calendar

Secular special days can also be great times to be intentional about connecting redemptively to people. Many churches are leveraging these days to serve people in ways that meet felt needs. Consider Valentine's Day, St. Patrick's Day, Mother's Day, Father's Day, July 4th, Canada Day, Halloween and Thanksgiving as spiritual harvest opportunities.

"Community" Calendar

Every community has special events that provide ways for churches to become known as valuable servants and community partners. Seasonal community festivals are potential times to implement the principle *"Where people congregate, we will operate."* Area schools, recreation and sports programs, city parks, hunting/fishing seasons can all provide options for churches to be seen as an important part of community life.

"Where people congregate, we will operate."

Serving in these ways develops relationships and continues nurturing receptivity among sphere of influence leaders. Churches don't always have to plan events to get people to come to them, we can go where people already are and demonstrate God's love in practical ways there!

"Celebration/Crisis" Calendar

People are more spiritually accessible in times of transition in their lives. Pay attention to birth, marriage or death announcements, those going through divorce or grief, people who have recently moved, people dealing with addiction. Churches that sensitively reach out and develop ministries to meet those needs will often find receptive people.

"Circumstance" Calendar

Occasionally, special things happen that are not on any of the other calendars we've mentioned. For example, the events of 9-11 were a circumstance where many people sought hope, truth and comfort. In a different vein, many churches leveraged the release of movies like "Fireproof" and "Courageous" as a great way to redemptively engage their communities. There may be other opportunities for churches to team up for special events in their area. It's a powerful witness to people outside the church to see different churches working together as God's team! Churches need to be ready to mobilize their efforts quickly to make the most of these circumstances for bringing Good News to people.

If you are planting a church, be especially sensitive and intentional about launching in a receptive season of your community's calendar. Often this is in the springtime leading up to Easter and in the fall as school begins, but pay attention to the unique dynamics of your local mission field.

How intentional are you about developing a "missional calendar"? When we are spiritually sensitive and also strategic in our efforts, we can improve harvest results. You can be intentional, incarnational and invitational in your ministry!

Discern Missional Partners

Studying your mission field redemptively and finding receptive "S*o*I*L" often leads to great missional partnerships! When you partner with a group or organization in your community, you don't always have to create or manage the program. You can just invest time and energy directly into people. You don't have to develop a new ministry. You can join someone else in his or her environment in a way that produces a win/win outcome.

When you simply join another group in a missional partnership, two networks of relationships are created: relationships with those we serve and those we serve with. Missional partnerships also include the people you take with you to serve. There are many unchurched people who are very receptive to doing community service, long before they might be open to attending church.

Who is Jesus calling you to serve with? There are many possibilities—community organizations, social service agencies, local schools, local businesses, nonprofits, other churches—every community has opportunities for missional partnerships. Who you choose to partner with is determined by a number of factors, including their receptivity, policies, the relational connections you have with them and the "OK" of the Holy Spirit. There are some organizations you may not feel comfortable with because of their priorities or values. However, remember that the Lord is sending you to be Good News to the people you serve with, not just the people you serve! Wisely discern where you can find *common ground for the common good* as you develop missional partners.

Another group to consider are unchurched people you have relationships with who are interested in serving. People are often looking for a cause bigger than themselves that makes a difference. As the people of your church talk about what they are doing out in the community with their friends, family, neighbors and co- workers, you will find interest and receptiveness in unexpected and rewarding ways!

Who are the people with whom the Lord is giving you favor, affinity and relationship? These become your Ministry Focus Group.

Pray about who you can invite to serve with you...and then ask them! Invitations to serve together can become bridges to salvation.

Think of those your church serves as potential ministry partners. As we serve, love, listen and pray intentionally, we will gain favor and build relationships with people. The Lord supernaturally connects who we are as God's Kingdom Team to those in our mission field who are receptive to Him. Although the Good News is for everyone, you will discern those with whom the Lord has given you favor, affinity and relationship. These people can be described as a "Ministry Focus Group" (MFG). Spiritual sensitivity leads to strategic ministry to those the Lord's been preparing for us to reach!

Blend together the insights from your intercession, intentional study, serving opportunities and God's divine appointments. Include people with whom you discover you share common interests and free time, values and beliefs, vocational issues or personal or community needs. Describe what your MFG looks like.

Develop Missional Bridges

Ministry activities require effort to become missional bridges. Always plan how you will leverage an activity to build bridges to Jesus and into your church. Plan each event with the next one in mind. The more bridges we build, the more people will cross over into life in Christ, fruitful relationships with others, and meaningful ministry. A ministry in your community should bridge to one at your church.

Here are some ways to create "missional bridges":

"Taste and See"—Plan small and large group opportunities for people to get to know you and your church's vision, values and mission. Let them "taste and see that the Lord is good…and our church is, too!"

"Go and Serve"—Go out (sometimes partnering with other community groups) to serve redemptively, demonstrating God's love in practical ways. This is where to deploy your ministry and

mission teams. Remember, "Where people congregate, we will operate."

"Learn and Grow"—Develop short-term seminars or groups to meet felt needs, usually four to six weeks long. These can be done inside or outside your church.

"Get to Know"—Develop creative ways for people to connect relationally. "Social" can be "spiritual," too! People want to experience life in community. As we do life together, we can see grace at work in each other.

These strategies do not need to be done sequentially. It's more important that they be done sensitively in order to leverage them for building ministry momentum. The key is always being intentional about the relationships they make possible.

As you develop your missional strategy in terms of who you will serve and who you will serve with, give yourself flexibility for "missional discovery." Experiment and field test to see what works and what doesn't. See where the Lord is blessing and join Him. Don't be afraid to change where you devote your missional energy.

COACH YOURSELF FORWARD

1. What insights did your gain from the word picture about "learning to play without the queen"? How can you apply these insights in your leadership conversations and your ministry planning?
2. As you process issues related to developing a missional calendar, what did you discover that helps you shape your missional game plan?
3. What events can we connect with in order to meet people where they already gather? What is on our community's calendar that should be seen as an opportunity to serve? Remember, "Where people congregate, we will operate."

4. What are your options in regard to missional partners in your community? God's partners may be surprising, so give Him room to work in relationships He gives you.

5. How will you equip others to invite their unchurched friends to join your church in serving your community?

6. What creative ways can you think of for "missional bridges" connecting others with God through ministry activities in and outside your church?

7. How will you be intentional about building momentum and connecting what you are doing outside the church with ministries inside the church? Remember to always leverage an event forward to the next events or redemptive opportunities.

FURTHER RESOURCES

Tangible Kingdom and *Tangible Kingdom Primer* (for small groups) by Hugh Halter and Matt Smay (Jossey-Bass, 2009)

Conspiracy of Kindness by Steve Sjogren (Regal Books, 2008)

101 Ways to Reach Your Community by Steve Sjogren (NavPress, 2000)

101 Ways to Help People in Need by Steve and Janie Sjogren (NavPress, 2002)

5 Things Any Congregation Can Do to Care for Others by Jason Cusick (Wesleyan Publishing House, 2009)

Mobilizing for Compassion: Moving People into Ministry by Robert Logan and Larry Short (Fleming H. Revell, 2004)

Heartbeat: How to Turn Passion into Ministry by Chip Arn (Xulon Press, 2011)

6

"Storytelling"

that Makes Good News Real

Over the next several weeks, Tom and Bill worked together with church leaders to implement the game plan out in their community. Although some struggled with and resisted the focus on reaching lost people and doing ministry out in the community, many others were energized and engaged. People who had been mostly inactive now found fresh ways to be included. The stories of what the Lord was doing through their service became a wonderful buzz throughout the church. Ideas for new ministries and teams arose from the discoveries and relationships they made.

"It's happening!" exclaimed Tom as they got together for their coaching visit. "I've had the privilege of bringing some of my neighbors to Christ. Some of them are beginning to come to church."

"That's awesome!" exclaimed Bill. "Nothing fuels my heart like seeing someone find life in Christ. I can see it in your eyes, too! How are things going overall as a church?"

"We're on a real learning curve," replied Tom. "Some things we tried didn't work out as we had hoped, but other doors are opening to us in supernatural ways. We're having opportunities to love and serve people in ways we'd prayed could happen... now it is! It's also been very humbling. At first, we tended to approach our service as things we were doing *for* people. But we have learned so much *from* the people we were serving that the Lord has changed our attitudes. Now, we are doing life *with* people, instead of just doing things *for* people. We're hearing their stories and finding ways to share our own stories in natural ways. We're enjoying new relationships and friendships. God is giving us increasing favor with our neighbors. Since we've become more intentional about building bridges into our mission field, it's making it easier to invite people back over those bridges to things we're doing at church.

The two fist-bumped in celebration. "Way to go, God!" exclaimed Bill. "How's it been going for your ministry buddies? I know you've been learning to coach each other for developing your own missional game plans. What are you learning from them?"

"As I've debriefed friends around the country, they have all personalized their own unique game plans. Yet, we are finding similar results," said Tom. "One of my friends described his experience as changing from being a 'professional minister' doing church work to a 'missional leader' leading a team of missionaries out into their mission field. It's transformational! The process your coaching is helping me develop is rippling through their ministries, too."

The Progression of Growing Skills:

Bill smiled. "It's amazing how the process unfolds itself, isn't it? Whether it's growing coaching

Unaware & unable
Conscious but uncomfortable
Comfortable & increasingly competent
Supernaturally natural

skills or missional ministry skills, we tend to follow a progression. First, we're *unaware and unable*...we don't know what we need to know and we don't know what to do. Next, we become *conscious, but uncomfortable*...we know what we should do, but we struggle to know how to do it. Then, we reach the point of being *comfortable and increasingly competent*...we know what to do and feel like we're getting good at it. The ultimate goal is to become *supernaturally natural*... we work hard to improve skills, but we are conscious that it all flows from the work of the Holy Spirit in and through us. What I heard you describe is how the Lord is empowering you to be supernaturally natural as a missional leader. I can see how much the Lord has grown you. I'll say it again: Way to go, God!"

Tom nodded humbly. "Thanks. I'm grateful for how the Lord has used you to help me grow. But, I've still got a long way to go!"

"We all do, brother," replied Bill. "Still, it's important to stop and see how far He's brought us sometimes. So, fellow missionary... what's the goal of our conversation today?"

"We need to work on the *storytelling* part of our missional pathway. Because we've been out making friendships, we are seeing more people come to church. We're finding out how true it is that many people are open to come to church if only someone they know and trust will just invite them. That's been thrilling! We've been asking our guests for their feedback about their experience at church...and..." Tom paused.

"And? What have you been learning?" asked Bill.

"Well, I think I understand what it is like for you as a missionary even more," said Tom. "We found out that things we take for granted about what we say and how we do church can be unfamiliar and even confusing for people who are not used to church. They really want to know Jesus, but sometimes it's like we're speaking a foreign language to them. I want our church to speak their language so we aren't hindering them from coming to Christ!"

Bill nodded. "I've had very similar experiences as a missionary. I had to learn to relate to others on their level and speak their language. When it came to introducing them to worship and the gospel, we had to learn how to translate the Good News for them, instead of making them interpret it for themselves… and there's a big difference. We didn't change the message of the Gospel, but we had to change how we communicated it."

An "aha" look came to Tom's face. "That's what we need to do better!" he exclaimed. "We need to adapt the way we do church with new people in mind. Instead of assuming that everyone knows what's going on, we'll have to be intentional about translating what we're doing so new people can understand and respond to Christ. The only barriers I want people to have to overcome in choosing Christ are the choices they make of their own freewill. So, how about if we focus on how we can share God's story better. Let's work on some translation skills!"

Bill laughed. "I love it! I wish more pastors and churches were working on that. I visit so many churches that, frankly, are not prepared for newcomers. Sometimes, what I see and hear makes me cringe. To hear a pastor like you who wants to be intentional about translating the Good News is music to my ears. So, let's get a picture of where you and your church are when it comes to becoming great storytellers. Who do we need to equip with good storytelling skills? In what ways are you doing a good job right now? In what ways do you need to pay attention to how the church presents itself and the gospel better?"

Tom nodded. "Good questions. Let's paint our picture of reality and then generate some options that we turn into our game plan."

Bill grinned. "You've got the G-R-O-W coaching plan down well! May I make an observation that might help our conversation further?"

"Sure," Tom said.

Bill continued, "A priority I've learned

We have to be intentionally incarnational *and* invitational to bring Jesus to people and people to Jesus!

as a missionary is to be both incarnational and invitational. It isn't enough for us to just do good things in Jesus' name. We have to be intentional about making sure we share the plan of salvation clearly and invite people to cross the line of faith and commit their lives to Christ. So, another question for you to consider is, how will you be intentional about being both incarnational *and* invitational to bring people to Jesus?"

"That's a great insight," returned Tom. "My ministry friends and I have been talking about very similar issues. Some of our younger leaders at church have been thrilled by how we are showing Jesus to people, while some of our older leaders are reminding me that our goal is still to see people saved. Let's make sure we're paying attention to both as we get to our action steps."

Together, Tom and Bill identified a number of areas that needed attention in their ministry. They realized that they needed to equip their people better to share their own story and the plan of salvation in a simple and natural way. They decided to ask some friends to act like "mystery shoppers" when they came to church and give feedback about how the church could be better prepared for new people. They also determined that they needed to look at how the church described itself through media and other means.

"We have to address our storytelling and translating in more ways than I would have guessed!" Tom said, as he looked at his action steps. "It's how we look, it's what we say, it's what people see and hear, it's considering all ages and stages of life...we can't take anything for granted."

"True...but you're developing a great game plan to help you improve," said Bill. "We're making great progress...and it's only going to get better for those we want to reach!"

The two leaders laid their game plan before the Lord, praying for His wisdom and favor and inviting Him to lead them. "Let Your

Kingdom come...let Your will be done here in us and through us as You've already mapped it out from heaven, Lord. We're here for Your purposes...we're all Yours...lead us according to Your plan!"

Translate His Story at Church

How we "tell the story"—in other words, our style of church and strategy for ministry—has to be shaped by listening, serving and relating. As we prayerfully discern the persons God is calling us to invest in for Kingdom purposes, we must learn how best to communicate the Good News to them effectively.

When people come to church, does your church translate for them, or do they have to interpret things for themselves? Think about the last time you went to a "new" place. Perhaps you came at the invitation of a friend, or you just wanted to check it out because something there interested you. What was the experience like? How easy was it for you to understand where to go and what to do? How welcome did others make you feel? How much did they "translate" things for you so you could understand what was going on? How much did you have to "interpret" without any help? What made you want to go back? What made you not want to go back?

Increasing numbers of people in our culture have little or no church or biblical background. They don't understand church "stuff" as we do, so everything is new to them. The key issue as we seek to tell the story of Jesus is to make sure we good translators—going out of our way to help others understand, appreciate and enter in, so they can meet Jesus at their level. Remember, what is familiar to us may be confusing to others. Be concerned about things like...

- *Verbiage and terms*—Even if words are biblical or theological, be sure to translate churchy language for unchurched people!
- *Unfamiliar spaces*—Do you have hosts and hospitality teams to welcome, guide and answer questions for

newcomers? Most new people decide whether they want to return within the first few minutes of their visit… before they even hear your church's music or listen to a message!

- **Signs and maps**—After people find your address, can they also find restrooms and children's classrooms?
- **Your church's "look" and "smell"**—What do people see and smell when they visit? How clean, fresh and inviting are we?
- **Worship style and patterns**—Tell new folks what you're doing and why.
- **Names of people and places**—Church people we know by first name—as in, "See Sue for more information," or "We'll meet over at the Smith's"—are unknown to new people!

The best compliment a church can receive from a visitor is, "It was like you were expecting me to come today!" Here are key questions:

- What redemptive analogy or biblical story best describes how to engage your Ministry Focus Group (MFG)?
- What would truly be "Good News" to our MFG? What would it look and sound like to them?
- What style of "church" will minister to our MFG most effectively? How can we make sure our church services are designed with new people in mind?
- How can we creatively, consistently and clearly communicate the Good News to our community, in order to bring people closer to a saving knowledge of Christ?
- How will we create intentional opportunities to invite people to commit their lives to Christ?

Tell Your Personal Story

"But in your hearts set apart Christ as Lord. Always be prepared to give an answer to anyone who asks you to give the reason for the hope that you have. But do this with gentleness and respect…." (I Peter 3:15 NIV)

"Devote yourselves to prayer with an alert mind and a thankful heart. Pray for us, too, that God will give us many opportunities to speak about his mysterious plan concerning Christ. That is why I am here in chains. Pray that I will proclaim this message as clearly as I should. Live wisely among those who are not believers, and make the most of every opportunity. Let your conversation be gracious and attractive so that you will have the right response for everyone." (Colossians 4:2-6 NLT)

We meet people at different places along their spiritual journey continuum. We've already learned that our first practice should be redemptive listening—the process of hearing their stories, sharing your story, and connecting them to His story! Everyone has a story to tell. The Lord will help you learn to share your story in a natural way that fits who you are. The Holy Spirit will supernaturally use your story to influence others in remarkable ways!

Make sure you take the time to listen to the stories of those you serve. As you do, you'll find the keys to their heart—their longings, wounds, dreams, broken places, needs. Share the parts of your story that connects to theirs. Find a way to share the story of Jesus that meets them on a heart level.

As Colossians 4:2-6 reminds us, it is a great honor to take the mystery out of knowing God. Here are basic ingredients for blending your story with God's story so that your friends can discover how He connects to their story, too.

- Before I met Jesus, my life was…

- I realized I needed Jesus when…

- I committed my life to Jesus by…

- Since I met Jesus, my life is…

- You can know Jesus, too, by…

Tell Your Church's Story

It's been said for a long time that "word of mouth" is by far the most effective form of marketing. The way a missional game plan helps you listen to, relate with, and serve others provides practical and natural ways for your church to create "word of mouth" opportunities for telling its story. Many churches have worked on a mission statement that describes their vision, values and strategy. Often these are only "in house" documents, which is important. However, it's also important to develop ways to "tell the story" of your church for those you want to invite to Christ and your fellowship. Think about how you can communicate your vision, values and mission in concise, energizing ways for unchurched people.

- **Vision**—paints a positive picture of what God is doing in and through your church—WHERE He is leading you.
- **Values**—describes your priorities—WHY you do what you do.
- **Mission**—states WHO you want to reach, WHAT their need are and HOW you are meeting those needs to bring them to Christ.

Remember, your mission field will shape these issues. If you can share your story in an energizing, memorable way in a sentence, you may invite longer conversations that build bridges to people.

Consider how you will "tell your story" on three levels:

- **Coffee cup or T-shirt**—your message in a simple, memorable sentence or phrase.
- **Elevator speech or Tweet**—your story in 10-15 seconds that invites further conversation.
- **Bullet points**—your vision, values and mission in an extended conversation, or as your present your church through your website, blogs or other media.

As we said, personal "word of mouth" conversations are the best, but there are many other means you can use to communicate your church's story. Consider various forms of media that fit best in your context: mailings, TV or radio spots, invite cards your people can hand out, billboards, website, social media, blogs, etc. There are many creative and often inexpensive ways to communicate!

The main issue is to make sure you are translating your church's story in ways that are interesting, energizing, inviting and memorable for the people on your mission field. Share your church's story! Share it often, share it well, and expect people to respond. Remember, they're waiting for us!

COACH YOURSELF FORWARD

1. When we talked about "translating" for new people, what issues did you identify that need your immediate attention?
2. What can you do to see your church's facilities, ministries, means of communication and services through the eyes of new people? How can you be intentional about that kind of evaluation in order to capture insights you need to address?
3. What action steps do you need to take to make your facilities and ministries more welcoming and understandable for new people?
4. How are you developing ways to include and connect new people to your church?
5. In what ways could you better equip the people of your church to share their story and God's story in simple, clear and natural ways?
6. How are you sharing your church's story with your community? In what ways can you be more clear, energizing and memorable?
7. Consider the many methods and means you can use to share your church's story. What are you currently doing?

What are some new possibilities? How will you integrate them?

FURTHER RESOURCES

Perfect Blend DVD and group study guide by Chris Conrad (Wesleyan Publishing House, 2009)

Five Things Anyone Can Do to Introduce Someone to Jesus by Chris Conrad (Wesleyan Publishing House, 2007)

Missing in America by Tom Clegg (Group Publishing, 2007)

Five Things Anyone Can Do to Help Their Church Grow by Phil Stevenson (Wesleyan Publishing House, 2007)

Becoming a Contagious Christian by Bill Hybels and Mark Mittleberg (Zondervan, 1996)

Knowing God booklet by Keith Drury (Wesleyan Publishing House, 2006)

A Good Start booklet by Ken Heer (Wesleyan Publishing House, 2003)

Your Next Step booklet by Ken Heer (Wesleyan Publishing House, 2003)

7

"*Spreading*"

Grace to New Places

"Bill, tell me again how you and your team planted churches in so many places," Tom said during their next coaching visit.

"I'd be glad to, but why do you ask?" replied Bill.

"The Lord's been stirring some new things in us as a team," said Tom. "We've been living out our missional game plan as a church, and God's been doing wonderful things in us and through us. You know what we've been doing out in our mission field. We've started a new service to help us reach more people right in our own building. We're a different church now! It's been more difficult and yet rewarding than we could have dreamed. Like the old slogan, missional ministry is the toughest job you'll ever love! It's been the greatest adventure in my leadership journey. As grateful as we are, we believe the Lord is calling us beyond our church to do more."

"How has the Lord been speaking to you?" Bill asked, intense interest on his face.

"He's speaking to us in several ways. He's increasing our hunger for more people to come to know Him. As people come to Christ, we find ourselves pleading with the Lord to trust us with even more souls. I find myself praying for our community like one of my ministry heroes, John Knox, used to pray for his nation: 'Give me Scotland, or I'll die!' The Lord s also stretching the way we see our mission field. There are some people who probably don't feel like our church is the best fit for them. What if we could start a ministry or new site or a new church that was designed for them? There are people who are now coming to our church who drive from a distance. It's hard for them to invite their neighbors to come so far. What if we started a church for them where they live? What if we could invest more intentionally in starting churches in places far from us, like the mission field you serve? We're starting to understand what John Wesley meant when he said 'The world is my parish.'"

"That's great, Tom!" Bill exclaimed, his face shining. "I've been praying for the Lord to expand your boundaries and increase your influence for Him. He's moving you toward ministry multiplication with an Acts 1:8 mindset."

"What do you mean?" asked Tom.

"It's a simple way to discern potential mission fields," Bill said. "When Jesus said He would send the Holy Spirit to give us supernatural power to be His witnesses, He identified four places. Remember what they were?"

"Jerusalem, Judea, Samaria and the ends of the earth," responded Tom. "What might they mean for us today?"

"Great question," said Bill. Grabbing a sheet of paper, he wrote:

- Jerusalem: people **like** us and **near** us

- Judea: people **like** us but **not near** us

- Samaria: people **not like** us but **near** us

- Ends of the earth: people **not like** us and **not near** us

"How does an Acts 1:8 mindset relate to what the Lord has been saying to you?" asked Bill.

"Wow... it fits perfectly!" exclaimed Tom. "That will really help us think about the potential scope of our missional ministry from a biblical but simple perspective. If the Lord is calling us to take His grace to new places, how can we do that? How could we use the principles that helped us design our game plan to do missional ministry in other places?"

"Is that what you want to focus on today?"

"Is that a rhetorical question?" teased Tom. "Let's go after it and see how we can do what the Lord's been saying to us!"

Together, Tom and Bill adapted the same missional pathway they had followed for Tom's church and coached themselves to a game plan that would equip their church to multiply its ministry in new ways and settings.

It wouldn't be the last time Tom coached his leaders through a similar process.

"Who"—Looking with an Acts 1:8 Mindset

> "But you will receive power when the Holy Spirit comes upon you, and you will be My witnesses in Jerusalem, in all Judea and Samaria and to the ends of the earth."(Acts 1:8 NIV)

An Acts 1:8 perspective allows leaders to engage in maximum missional ministry! Beyond our initial Ministry Focus Group (read that as "Jerusalem"), the Lord wants us to pay attention to other opportunities He is preparing. Using Acts 1:8 as a missional grid, prayerfully consider new possibilities for spreading grace to new places. Who are the people your local church has the greatest potential to impact for Christ?

> *Jerusalem*—People **near** us and **like** us. They may come to our church, as we will find ways to build redemptive bridges to them.

Judea—People **like** us but not **near** us. They would come to our church, but live too far away. What kinds of ministries or new churches could we start to reach them where they live?

Samaria—People **near** us but not **like** us. They may not connect easily to our church, but we could start another ministry, service or church for them, even though it's close to our own church. What people groups or special opportunities might fit "Samaria" ministry in your situation?

Ends of the earth—People not **like** us and not **near** us. Increasingly, ministry is blending local and global to become "glocal." Consider how you can partner with missionaries in other parts of the world to plant churches and other missional initiatives. Work with your denomination's global missions team to discover opportunities that might fit your church.

"Where"—Following the Spirit's Lead

Discerning where the Lord might have your church launch a new initiative takes prayer and strategic wisdom. Along with your leaders, consider these questions:

- For whom is the Lord giving us a burden?
- Who is a person of peace through whom we can gain access to more unreached people?
- Where is the Lord giving us favor and open doors?

Sometimes we may desire to go in a particular direction, but the Lord restrains or redirects us. Acts 16:4-10, prompts us to ask, "Where might the Lord be giving us an unexpected "Macedonian call?"

Then they went from town to town, instructing the believers to follow the decisions made by the apostles and elders in Jerusalem. So the churches were strengthened in their faith and grew larger every day. Next Paul and Silas traveled through the area of Phrygia and Galatia, because the Holy Spirit had prevented them from preaching the word in the province of Asia at that time. Then coming to the borders of Mysia, they headed north for the province of Bithynia, but again the Spirit of Jesus did not allow them to go there. So instead, they went on through Mysia to the seaport of Troas. That night Paul had a vision: A man from Macedonia in northern Greece was standing there, pleading with him, "Come over to Macedonia and help us!" So we decided to leave for Macedonia at once, having concluded that God was calling us to preach the Good News there. (Acts 16:4-10 NLT)

- Where are clusters of people from our church living that might indicate a possible new ministry location or initiative?
- What invitations have we received from our missional partners?
- Who has the Lord brought to our church that could become missionaries to lead new initiatives?
- What are we hearing from our leaders? Pay special attention to what the Lord is birthing in their hearts!
- How could we join the bigger team of churches in our district, denomination or mission agency as a partner?

"When"—Ministry Flow Charts and Timelines

As you do the work of spiritual discernment, you'll also need to do the work of strategic planning. Designing a ministry flow chart and timeline will help you organize and optimize new ministry designs.

A ministry flow chart is a diagram of major ministries, programs, teams and events.

- It shows each ministry in relation to the others.
- It shows the logical sequence by which people become connected and involved step by step.
- It shows the intended result of ministry involvement.

- It is useful to show what ministries might be missing, especially missional teams.
- It shows how your missional game plan begins out in your mission field, makes disciples, and then deploys disciples and teams back into your mission field!
- It has missional multiplication in mind!

Here's an exercise for evaluating and expanding your church's current ministries. List each major ministry team, event, or program that you currently have or plan to have on a Post It™ note. If you are starting a new service, ministry or church, plan with your intended outcome in mind.

Organize the Post It™ notes sequentially on a poster board to show step-by-step how you will connect to unchurched people, lead them to Christ, grow them in leadership and equip them as reproducing leaders. Make sure an intentional disciple-making pathway emerges.

If designing a new ministry, put dates on the pathway to make it a timeline. Although you will be more "checkpoint" than calendar driven in your planning, set a date in the future for the new ministry to begin and work backwards from this launch date to establish the sequence necessary for a successful launch. Review your work as a team. Add any essential missing ministries, teams or events.

Identify any unnecessary ministry activities and set them aside. Look for "bottlenecks and disconnects"—points where progress can easily be interrupted or hindered. Think about what level of commitment is required for each step. What additional strategies might be needed for growing and equipping people? What communication and relationships are essential for moving people from one level of commitment and involvement with one another?

Now, connect the notes with arrows to form a pathway and timeline for your game plan. Give yourself permission to adapt your plan as situations warrant. Put everything at the disposal and direction of the Holy Spirit. Dream big. Work hard. Stay dependent. Pray much.

Expect! Developing a game plan for missional ministry is one of the most rewarding things you can do. Cover everything with prayer. Keep at it. And watch God work through you!

COACH YOURSELF FORWARD

1. Review your mission field from an Acts 1:8 perspective. What possibilities can you discover?
2. In what ways is the Lord calling you to spread grace to new places and people?
3. Prayerfully review the questions related to discerning new places for ministry. What further questions could you add? What is the Lord making clear to you?
4. Step back and take a look at your church's "Ministry Flow Chart." What issues might you need to address, especially where there are gaps that hinder the flow of ministry?
5. What area is most important to address first?
6. What new initiative is the Lord calling you to pursue? Design a timeline with the launch of the new ministry or church in mind. Work backward from your launch date and develop your ministry flow chart.
7. How big is your mission field now?

FURTHER RESOURCES

Movements That Change the World by Steve Addison (IVP, 2011)

Planting a Missional Church by Ed Stetzer (Broadman & Hulman Academic, 2006)

Five Things Anyone Can Do to Plant a New Church by Phil Stevenson, *www.wesleyan.org/ecg/resources_church_planter_resources*

Church Planting Resource Manual by Chris Conrad and Jerry Pence, *www.wesleyan.org/ecg/resources_church_planter_resources*

Afterword

The time came for Bill and his family to return to their ministry assignment overseas. He and Tom got together over coffee one last time at their usual place to reflect on what the Lord had done over the months that they walked together. As they did, they gave the thanks and glory to Him.

"What began as an invitation to coffee and conversation became a life changing coaching relationship for me," said Tom. "I longed to bring Jesus to our community, so people could know how much He loves them, but didn't know how. But the missional game plan coming out of our coaching relationship changed the course of our church and its influence in our community. Now, Jesus is famous in so many more ways. So many have come home to the Father in the last few months! Now it's not uncommon for me to hear, 'If your church wasn't here, it would be a huge loss to our community.'"

Bill smiled and nodded. "I can't tell you how grateful I am for what God is doing in my own hometown and home church. It's been an honor to work with you. We can't meet like this for coffee anymore, but we can still stay connected. I'm glad we live in a day when missionaries have email and Skype!"

Tom agreed. "Let's keep in touch. I still want your coaching from time to time. And, I'll see you when we bring a short-term team over to work with you in your mission field!"

"Can't wait," grinned Bill. "I may not be your coach in the same way, but now we're friends and fellow missionaries."

"Yup...and I'm not just a pastor anymore!" laughed Tom. "And I have you to thank for that."

"We both have Him to thank for that, and so much more," replied Bill. "Let's tell Him so."

They did.

Bill returned to his mission field. He had continued to coach leaders there, even while he was back home, and their ministries had grown during his absence. Multiplying more disciples, leaders and churches, they had even begun sending missionaries to other nations.

Tom went for more coach training and grew skills for equipping other leaders. Coaching became a primary way he approached ministry leadership in his church. He now coaches leaders all around the country, seeking to bless them, as Bill had blessed him.

Tom's ministry buddies discovered that the principles for developing a missional game plan could be applied in many settings. Intentional, missional concentration made a huge difference in their work. As they shared principles they learned as a result of Tom's coaching with their own networks of friends, there was a wonderful ripple effect. Many other new ministries and churches were birthed. The dream of ministries that multiplied disciples, leaders, ministries and churches became reality.

A Personal Challenge

It's our dream that coaching conversations like you saw with Bill and Tom will take place all the time, among all kinds of leaders. As more of us equip one another with an A*C*T*N plan for assessing, coaching, training and networking, we believe that healthy churches will follow the direction of the Holy Spirit and develop their own game plans for intentional missional ministry. Church planting teams will also make a missional game plan an integral part of their ministry strategy. As a result, our vision to "fulfill the Great Commission in the Spirit of the Great Commandment" will thrive and flourish. Local churches, groups of churches, and denominations will make their contribution to Kingdom work in our generation and a new generation of leaders will rise up to make Kingdom history after us.

John Wesley's words still summon us across the centuries: "You have nothing to do but save souls." Let's respond enthusiastically, "Then let everything we do be about saving souls!"

Appendix A
Coaching Guideline

*Coach*_____ *Leader* _____ *Date* _____

Remember the Seven Habits of a Great Coach—Listen, Care, Celebrate, Strategize, Train, Disciple, Challenge

As you open—Listen...Care...Celebrate—personal and ministry updates

Where is God working? (Clarify Calling, Cultivate Character, Create Community, Connect to Culture)

Goal—(What is the purpose of our visit?)
    What are we going to focus on today? What result would you like to get from our visit today?

Reality—(Paint a picture of what's really happening)
    What's really going on? Where is God at work? What's working? What's not? In what ways have you addressed this issue? What have you been learning? What other information do we need to know that will help us address this issue?

"Great Commandment Listening" (from Matthew 22:37-39)—
Listen for what is going on in the:
* *"Heart"* (spirit)—What have you been hearing from the Lord? What does your heart say?
* *"Soul"* (emotions)—What have you been feeling about this?
* *"Mind"* (reason)—What are the facts? What is the most reasonable way to look at this?
* *"Strength"* (physical)—How is your health? How much time, energy and resources will you need?

- *"Others as yourself"* (other's views)—What would your spouse say about this? Other leaders and friends? If they were in your shoes, what would they say?

Options—(What are our possibilities)

Develop a list of ideas. Challenge obstacles by asking, "What if we overcame that?" Keep asking, *"What else?" "In what ways could we..."*

Will—(What will you do? What action steps will you take? What is your game plan?) Set "S*M*A*R*T goals—Specific, Measurable, Achievable, Relevant, Time-bound

- What do you choose to do?
- Where does this fit into the big picture, our master plan?
- When will you begin?
- When will you complete this?
- Who else needs to know?
- Who else will you need? (Think about God's team)
- What resources will be required?
- What other issues do we need to consider in our plan?

Wrapping up...

- What was most helpful to you from our visit today?
- When will we have our next coaching visit?
- Let's pray!

Appendix B
Scriptural Insights for Missional Ministry

<u>**Joshua: God's Plan for His People to Take His Promised Land**</u>

The mission: acquire and dwell in the land God promised His people. The plan: designed by the Lord, implemented by His leaders as they deployed God's tribes. Military leaders still use the book of Numbers to train soldiers today. The plan had to be adapted to different settings and changing scenarios.

- Every new ministry and church begins in the heart of God.
- God's promises become reality as the Spirit of God leads His people and they follow in obedient faith!

1. **God Calls a Leader to Take His People Into "The Land." (1:1-10)**

   - Moses mentored Joshua. Young leaders need this ministry!
   - God wants to first reveal Himself to the leader before He reveals His call. God's mandate is undergirded by His promises. The call flows from God's character being developed in the heart of the leader.
   - God's leader must be a man or woman of the Word, who lives "promise to promise," not "problem to problem." The attitude of the leader makes all the difference.

2. **God Compliments His Call by Confirmation from Others. (1:11-18)**

   - God calls a "Ministry Team" to support and follow the leader. No vision can be accomplished alone.
   - Different people will have differing roles in fulfilling the vision, but all are important.

3. **Concentrate on "The Land"—Do Spiritual "Recon." (2:1-24)**

   - Get to know people in the land—they know their area best!
   - See through God's eyes...find the "redemptive gifts" of the land and also the spiritual strongholds.

- Thank God for the "first fruits" of your ministry. "Rahabs" are waiting for you to come!

4. **Complete Consecration Brings Cleansing So We Can Fulfill the Call. (3:1-13; 5:1-12)**

- Pure hearts allow God to show His power.
- When "you've never been this way before," complete dependence on God is vital.

5. **Confirming Signs—God's Visible Affirmation of His Call! (3:14-4:24)**

- God presents a challenge—"a flooded Jordan"—and asks us to step out in obedient faith.
- Our obstacles become God's opportunities!
- God's first "confirming signs" to the leader and the people become an exciting part of their future "faith story."

6. **Commence by Addressing Strategic Strongholds. (5:13-27)**

- Focus on worship before warfare. Strategic intercession is essential!
- Get a fresh revelation of Jesus. Continually yield to His Lordship...do what He's blessing!
- Even if God's leading appears "foolish," obey and watch God bring down the walls!

7. **Courageously Deal with "Sin in the Camp." (7:1-26)**

- Overconfidence from past victories can breed prayerlessness.
- Hidden sin in a leader's life affects the spiritual climate of the entire group.
- Spiritual defeat can bring discouragement and doubt.
- Joshua struggled with "the death of the dream." Most every leader reaches a similar point.
- God will often allow the dream to "die" so He can resurrect it purified!

- Spiritual leaders must be willing to deal decisively with sinful conduct.
- Don't be afraid to lose some people to keep the dream pure. Never compromise eternal values for the sake of temporary expediencies.

8. **Commit Again to Covenant Priorities After Difficult Circumstances. (8:1-29)**
   - Make prayer a top priority again!
   - Get back to following God's plans.
   - Corporately restate the call and reinforce the primacy of God's Word.

9. **Careful! Beware of Deception. (9:1-27)**
   - Lack of prayer = lack of discernment. Satan can be very subtle in diverting our attention.
   - Seek good counsel from others before making major decisions.
   - Allowing ourselves to be deceived damages God's work.

10. **Challenge Demonic Coalitions. (10:1-12:24)**
    - Satan will sometimes come at you with a full-scale frontal attack, seeking to overwhelm you.
    - Dedicate the situation to God. Go to God first....pray! PRAY!
    - Dare to try something different at God's direction. He often tailors His strategy to your specific situation.
    - Do what you can do, then expect divine help.
    - Deal thoroughly with enemies...allow no demonized issues to remain.

11. **Conquer "The Land" Geographically and Strategically. (13:1-14:5)**
    - "See" the land as a divine inheritance! God has given it to you to extend His Kingdom!
    - Divide the land geographically.
    - Reduce it into manageable areas.

- Assign leaders to care for each area.
- Delegate authority.
- Divide and conquer.
- Don't try to take the land all at once.
- Take good care of spiritual leaders.

12. **Cherish and Nourish Pioneers and Faith-filled Leaders. (14:6-15)**
   - Praise God for "Calebs!" They are far too rare. If God brings them, give them "mountains" to conquer!
   - Honor visionaries and warriors.
   - Respect women's requests and allow them to lead. (15:17-19; 17:34)

13. **Consistency and Faithfulness—the Keys to Long-Term Ministry. (16-22)**
   - You won't win everyone, but stay faithful to the task. (16:10; 17:12-17; 18:1-10)
   - Challenge people to keep taking ground for God. (17:12-17)
   - Always have "safe places"—cities of refuge. (20:1ff)
   - Keep looking to God and praising Him. (21:43-45)
   - Bless those who have served well. (22:1-6)

14. **Conflict Resolution—Vital to Effective Leadership. (22:10-34)**
   - Most conflict comes from misconceptions and miscommunication more than bad motives.
   - Don't assume and accuse—get the facts first! (22:11-20)
   - Get both sides of the story. (22:21-28)
   - Be willing to change your opinion. (22:30-34)
   - Keep the vision a central priority, not personalities.
   - Healthy conflict resolution usually brings stronger relationships.

15. **Carrying On—Transfer Ownership of the Call and the Vision. (23-24)**
   - Remember, rejoice in and refocus on God—His call and His accomplishments.

- Reissue the call and reconfirm the vision.
- Renew covenant commitments.
- Revere Godly leaders...heroes of the faith deserve our respect and honor.

Acts: God's Multiplication Manual

Apostles and disciples of the early church were the first to live out the Great Commission strategy with the supernatural anointing and authority of the Holy Spirit. The combination of sanctified love from a pure heart, spiritual authority to defeat Satan's strategies and supernatural power for miracles made biblical multiplication an amazing reality. In the Book of Acts, we can see the principles that made such multiplication possible.

1. **"A Rushing Mighty Wind...the POWER for Multiplication"**
   - The Holy Spirit's purity and power—the essential for ministry. (1:8-2:4)
   - The Resurrected Jesus—the Risen Lord IN and THROUGH His people. (Acts 4:13)

2. **"The Building was Shaken...PRAYER and Multiplication"**
   - Whatever the need, they went to God first. Prayer was the priority. (Acts 2, 4, 13)
   - Worship and waiting—dependence on God for everything.
   - Importance of strategic intercession.

3. **"Let Your Kingdom Come...the PERSPECTIVE of Multiplication"**
   - A Kingdom perspective—give your best. (13:1ff)
   - Kingdom vs. empire. It's not about us building our church as a personal empire; it's about God's team working together to build His Kingdom so He gets all the glory.
   - All churches are involved...this is not only about planting new churches...the focus was expanding the Kingdom through new *and* existing churches.

4. **"To the Ends of the Earth...the PASSION of Multiplication"**
   - From local to global—Jerusalem, Judea, Samaria, to the ends of the earth. (Acts 1:8)

- Divine appointments—letting the Spirit lead to receptive places and people. (17:2ff)

5. **"No Other Name…the PRIORITY of Multiplication"**
   - Preach Christ—our intrinsic motivation. This is highlighted twelve times throughout Acts.
   - Unless evangelism is at the core, our efforts may be illegitimate.

6. **"If This is God, You Can't Stop Them…the POSSIBILITIES of Multiplication"**
   - The reality of risk…and importance of persistent, risk-taking faith. (Acts 4)
   - The importance of flexibility. (Acts 10)

7. **"We Must Obey God Rather Than Men…the PROBLEMS of Multiplication"**
   - Reality, ramifications and reactions. The effect of opposition turned out to be positive at every turn. Use problems as a judo move…use the weight of the opponent against them. (Acts 16)
   - Satanic opposition, religious legalism, struggle over resources and methods, church leadership issues, territorialism, persecution and prison can all be obstacles to multiplication.
   - If the Church did not heed the call to multiply, God allowed persecution.

8. **"I'm Going…Not Knowing What Awaits Me…the PERSEVERANCE of Multiplication"**
   - Many points where the church felt like giving up…their reaction made the difference.
   - "Death of a dream"—there are times when God allows our dream to die so we can refocus on the Dream Giver and His plans.
   - "In irons/doldrums"—our disappointments can become God's divine appointments. (Acts 16)

9. **"Dedicate...For the Special Work I Have for Them...the PARTNERSHIP of Multiplication"**

   - Leadership development facilitated expansion—Aquila and Priscilla, Apollos, Barnabas, Luke, etc.
   - Gift utilization and empowerment—Acts 6. Phillip and Stephen are examples of allowing others to serve according to their gifts. Later, Phillip's daughters served according to their gifts.
   - Think T*E*A*M—everyone is a minister, not just the superstars. We all make vital contributions!

10. **"Come Over and Help Us...the PLACEMENT of Multiplication"**

    - Divine appointments and re-appointments—the Macedonian call, sensitivity to the Spirit. (Acts 16)
    - Cultural relevance—Mars Hill (Acts 17), positioning our ministry to reach people where they are.
    - Keep your eyes on what's going on around you... allow the Lord to deploy people where He wants them. (Acts 13:1-4)

11. **"It Seems Good to the Holy Spirit and to Us...the PROMOTION of Multiplication"**

    - Leaders can bless or squelch what God is doing. (Acts15)
    - It's not just what we are saying...it's how we say it!
    - Building shared vision is vital for united ministry.
    - Communication takes place on many levels:
      a. Ruling elders to pioneers and young churches. (Acts 15)
      b. Peter sharing vision with the community. (Acts 2)
      c. Paul and Barnabas—personal. (Acts 15)
      d. Gospel going to Jerusalem, Samaria, and beyond to new people groups.

12. **"Then the Church Grew in Numbers and Enjoyed a Time of Peace...the PLEASURE of Multiplication"**

    - All churches are blessed by multiplication. (Acts 9:31)
    - God's pleasure in seeing His Great Commandment and Commission being fulfilled.

- "...Proclaiming the Kingdom of God with all boldness and teaching about the Lord Jesus Christ" (Acts 28:30) *and the adventure continues!*

(Bill Malick and Tim Roehl)

Luke 9 and 10: Jesus Strategy for Reaching New Communities

One of the greatest challenges we face is how to bring Good News to our community and region. Jesus sent His disciples into communities as advance teams for His Kingdom to come. As we watch Jesus send His disciples into ministry, we find His keys for Kingdom ministry...

1. He Sends Us Empowered and Equipped (Luke 9:1-17)
   A. He sends us...we have an *apostolic* commission (9:1,2). Never forget Who sends us!
   B. He empowers us...His provides *abundant ability* ("power") to deal with any situation in both the spiritual and physical *arenas* (9:1).
   C. He *authorizes* us and gives us Kingdom jurisdiction to act in His name when we come (9:1).
   D. He gives us a message to *announce*—the King is here and His Kingdom is come (9:2).
   E. He tells us where to *activate* His power first—meet people's felt and physical needs (9:2).
   F. Our ministry will *attract* some, *antagonize* others and *amaze* others as we show them Jesus (9:4,5,6,7-17).
   G. We must balance intense *activity* with intimate time *alone* with Jesus (9:10).

2. His Strategy of Evangelism Engagement (10:1-10)
   A. Evangelism always *starts* and is *sustained* with prayer (10:1,2).
   B. We are to be *"street smart"* and keep it *simple* (10:3,4).
   C. *Speak* peace to people with an attitude of blessing (10:5,6). Lost people are not our enemy! God wants to express His love to them through us!

D. Fellowship—*Share* life with them (10:7,8). Enter their world.

E. *Seek* to meet their physical needs. Don't be afraid to trust the Lord for His miraculous intervention (10: 9).

F. *Share* the Good News of God's Kingdom salvation (10:9,10). "God's Kingdom is right on your doorstep!"

3. Be Sensitive to the Lost!

Here's a "Top Ten List" that describes what the lost are looking for from us as Christians...

10. I don't care how much you know until I know how much you care.

9. Have compassion on me. Don't condemn me because my life's a mess.

8. Ask "permission" to tell me about God, don't just push Him on me. Talk *with* me, not *at* me. Listen to me. Find out about my world before you expect me to be interested in yours.

7. Use words I can understand.

6. Have a sense of humor! I want Christianity that can be enjoyed, not endured.

5. Don't focus on your church. Labels don't mean much to me. I'm looking for people who live like they really love God. Chances are I've been burnt or bored in church in the past.

4. Don't just tell me about your faith; show me your faith by serving others in love.

3. Take your time. Don't tell me everything at once. Give me time to let God work in my life.

2. Tell me how God can make a difference in my daily life, not just at church on Sunday. If I'm going to be a Christian, I want it to work in real life.

1. Make Jesus real to me. Show me simply how to know Him from His Word, and chances are I'll want to know Him, too. After all, I really do want to go to Heaven.

Appendix C
"Spy Teams" To Help You Discern God's Missional Game Plan for Your Church

As you seek to discern God's vision, values and mission for your church, a great strategy is to "spy out the land" to see where God is at work and join Him. Your mission is to ask questions, listen carefully, discern the lessons prayerfully and develop plans strategically.

The "History" Team—Looking Back
Why is important to review your church's history?
1. It gives *perspective.* You'll understand better...
   - why your church was <u>planted</u>,
   - who the <u>pioneers</u>/heroes were who risked obeying God,
   - what <u>priorities</u> motivated them,
   - what <u>problems</u> they faced and overcame,
   - what <u>promises</u> God gave them to help trust Him,
   - what <u>plans</u> they prayed through in the church's early days.
2. It gives *permission.* We often gain permission for our future from the lessons of our past! What risk-taking faith and obedience did your church's forefathers demonstrate that you could emulate?

Key Questions for the "History" Team
1. Why did your church begin? Who were the pioneers/risk-takers for God? How did your church begin? What were significant factors in your church's beginning? What can you learn from them?
2. When were your church's "glory days?" What did they look like? What was God doing in your midst? How did your people respond? What can you learn from them?

3. When were some of your church's "groaning days" when you went through difficult or lean times? What was happening? What were the factors that led to those times? What can you learn from them?

4. As you look at your church's potential and problems today, ask yourself, "Given the decisions they made then, what do we think those pioneers would have done with this issue?"

The "Community" Team—Looking Around

Why is important to see what is happening in your community?

1. It helps us discern the *"spiritual climate"* of your area. It is vital to see the big picture of what God is doing in your region in order to best find your place on God's Kingdom team. What are the "besetting sins" of your area—areas of visible pain and spiritual captivity? These often show us God's "redemptive opportunities" for ministry.

2. It helps you find the *"people of peace"* in your area who have significant influence with others. Sometimes they have positions of formal power. Some may be "informal" leaders without title, but with great wisdom and influence. Learning from them and gaining their favor is vital, often opening whole networks of people you can serve for Christ.

3. It helps you discern your *"opportunities and obstacles"* as you seek to reach others for Christ. What strongholds of sin hold people back from knowing Jesus? What redemptive gifts does Jesus want to release to set people free? What needs could you meet? What kinds of people aren't being reached? What "open doors" can you discover for ministry?

Key Questions for the "Community" Team

1. *What can you learn as you check the "S*o*I*L" (Sphere of Influence Leaders) in your community?*
   Develop a list and set up appointments with key leaders in various spheres of influence such as:

a. *Education*—school leaders
b. *Law Enforcement*—police chief, sheriff, etc.
c. *Government*—mayor, city/county officials, city planners, etc.
d. *Spiritual leaders*—pastors and parachurch leaders...our Kingdom teammates
e. *Business leaders*—Chamber of Commerce, Rotary, etc.
f. *Social service agencies*
g. *Media*—publishers, radio/TV, etc.
h. *Subcultures*—leaders in niche groups like partiers, bikers, ethnic groups, etc.
i. *Realtors and builders*
j. *"People of peace"*—those who have influence in the area whether they have a "title" or not and can open doors to large networks of relationships. Other leaders may tell you to talk to them. They may have lived in your area for a long time and seen changes the community has gone through.
k. The *"Bishop"*—the most influential spiritual leader of the area to learn from and get his blessing.
l. *"Divine appointments"*—watch for people God sends to you!

Here's a sample survey you can use with these "sphere of influence" leaders. Remember, be gracious and be brief. If they appear interested and want to give you more time, take advantage of their generosity and learn much.

1. How would you describe this area to a new person just moving in? What are its greatest strengths?
2. From your position as a leader of influence in this area, what do you see as its greatest needs?
3. What are some ways a church that wants to be a servant to our area could partner with agencies like yours to help others?
4. What advice would you give me as a new spiritual leader in our community?

5. Who else would you recommend that I talk to that could help me learn more?
6. How can I pray for you or your family? How can we serve you?
7. Thank you for your time! May we keep you updated on our progress?

What kinds of people groups live in your area? Who are you best suited to reach for Christ? (Ministry Focus Group) Who is reaching them for Christ? Ask, "How would we design our ministry if we were to take this people group seriously?"

The "Congregational" Team—Looking Within
Excellent resources for discerning your church's strengths and needs are the Church Health Profile (*www.churchhealthprofile.com*) or the Natural Church Development (NCD) survey. Let your scores serve as a reference point and ministry resource. Make sure your prayer warriors are saturating everything with prayer!

Key Questions for the "Congregational" Team
1. What dreams and expectations do the people of your church have for your ministry? How can you connect individual dreams with the bigger vision of your church?
2. What gifts do you see among the people of your church? How can they best be utilized to reach the lost and build up the Body of Christ?
3. What are your church's greatest strengths? How can you leverage them to reach more people?
4. Look over your church's facilities. What changes may be needed in order to best serve the people God has called you to reach?
5. What new ministries may be needed to help you accomplish the vision God is giving you?

6. What trends are you noticing in your church? What can you learn from them? How could you address them most wisely?

The "Kingdom" Team—Looking at God's Team

Your church is only one part of the "Kingdom Team" of churches and leaders God is raising up to reach your area for Christ. By learning what He is doing in other churches and ministries, you can best discern His "Kingdom niche" for your church. Have members of this team visit other churches in your area and talk with the leaders of those churches.

<u>Key Questions for the "Kingdom" Team</u>
1. What are some of your general observations about the health of the other ministries in your area? What are they doing that is having the biggest impact for Christ?
2. What needs are not being met by the other ministries in your area that your church could seek to provide?
3. How can you partner with other ministries in your area to make the most impact for the Lord?
4. How can you bless other ministries in your area?

Bringing It All Together...

After all the Spy Teams have "scouted out the land," come back together and have each share their findings. List them on Post It pads across a wall in this order...

<u>History</u>   <u>Congregational</u>   <u>Community</u>   <u>Kingdom</u>

As each Spy Team shares their findings, have the whole group summarize the main insights. Then, review again the findings of the Congregational and Community Spy Teams. What connections can you see between who you are as a church and needs/opportunities in your community you might be able to address in Jesus' name? What ministries might you develop to meet those needs and bring people to Christ?

In light of what you have learned and discerned from "scouting out the land," what are the next steps you can take as a church? Make some clear action steps stated as S*M*A*R*T goals:

- **S**pecific
- **M**easureable
- **A**chievable
- **R**elevant
- **T**ime bound

Appendix D
Mission and Ministry Team Worksheet

Mission Teams	Ministry Teams
Developed from study of our mission field	Developed from study of our church's health
Designed to release redemptive gifts to community	Designed to release gifts, skills and passion of Body
Dedicated to ministry opportunities	Done mainly inside of church
Done mainly outside of church	Discerns opportunities for missional expression